PAWPRINTS ALL OVER ME

C.E. "Stan" STANDLEY

To Linda —
It's all true. I hope
you enjoy this!
Best wishes
Stan
02/21/04

Printed in Victoria, Canada

National Library of Canada Cataloguing in Publication

Standley, C. E. "Stan", 1945-
    Pawprints all over me / C.E. "Stan" Standley.
ISBN 1-55395-747-4
    I. Title.
SF426.2.S73 2003   636.7   C2003-900621-2

TRAFFORD

This book was published *on-demand* in cooperation with Trafford Publishing.
On-demand publishing is a unique process and service of making a book available for retail sale to the public taking advantage of on-demand manufacturing and Internet marketing. **On-demand publishing** includes promotions, retail sales, manufacturing, order fulfilment, accounting and collecting royalties on behalf of the author.

Suite 6E, 2333 Government St., Victoria, B.C. V8T 4P4, CANADA

Phone	250-383-6864	Toll-free	1-888-232-4444 (Canada & US)
Fax	250-383-6804	E-mail	sales@trafford.com
Web site	www.trafford.com	TRAFFORD PUBLISHING IS A DIVISION OF TRAFFORD

HOLDINGS LTD.

Trafford Catalogue #03-0110   www.trafford.com/robots/03-0110.html

10   9   8   7   6   5   4   3

To all those dogs who were never allowed to be more than "just dogs"

ACKNOWLEDGEMENTS

There are numerous people who assisted either knowingly or unwittingly, directly or indirectly in the writing of this book; the words would not have appeared without their input or assistance. Sue Thomas of Camelot Kennels started the ball rolling by pointing us in the right direction. Judy Colan of Colsidex Kennels provided advice and other valuable assistance. Virginia Alexander and Jackie Isabell, the authors of *Weimaraner Ways*, produced an incredible book which provides so much information and advice on every conceivable aspect of Weimaraners. Paul and Kristen Logan proofed, critiqued and asked the hard questions.

There are also five dogs that have enriched our lives and provided the impetus for this book: Hilde, Blade, Lulu, Star and Eva. Each holds a special place in our hearts.

Finally, there is a dog from my past, one that never truly received the appreciation that he deserved. And maybe that is why we now have three dogs. Ultimately, he provided the real inspiration for this book. Buster, you are still missed.

FORWARD

It had been a really nice evening: dinner and a movie followed by a leisurely drive home. Pulling into the driveway, we reflected on the relaxing effect that had replaced the tense, hectic pace of that day...actually that entire week. The discussion continued as we worked our way toward the front door. Finally, I unlocked the door and Bobbie entered the house first. She froze and I heard her gasp followed by, "Oh, no!"

I pushed past her and saw a sight that was almost beyond description; the living room was in shambles!

Torn cloth and chunks of foam from our new sofa covered the floor. Magazines from the coffee table were also strewn about the room. We were both stunned and speechless as we surveyed the devastation that extended into the kitchen and into the dining room. How could someone do this? WHY would anyone do this? What were they searching for?

And then reality set in: EVA. That dog REALLY needs a hobby!

.......it wasn't always like this.

Some of our close friends cannot understand the bond between humans and their dogs. "They're just dogs" is a common phrase that we hear. Oh, no, far more than that...they are family members and their place in the family is not diminished by the fact that they have four legs instead of two. Many dog owners never elevate their canine friends above "just dog" status; I feel sorry for them and for their dogs. This book is about the very special side of canine ownership and about a very special breed. We have made lots of mistakes in the course of raising our dogs. On the other hand, we have had many wonderful experiences with our "gray ghosts" and look forward to many more.

So make yourself comfortable and enjoy what we hope is light, easy reading that will bring a smile to your face and warmth to your heart.

PAWPRINTS
ALL OVER ME

"He is your friend, your partner, your defender, your dog.
You are his life, his love, his leader. He will be yours,
faithful and true, to the last beat of his heart. You owe
it to him to be worthy of such devotion."

- Unknown -

Chapter 1

Buster

I grew up on a farm near Alvin, Texas; our family raised cattle and farmed rice. Our pets consisted of a few cats and several dogs over the years. A dog was the companion of a small boy and that usually extended to adulthood. Dogs were dogs...they helped out on the farm. Virtually every farm had at least one dog. That's the way it was.

Buster was a mixed breed male who was one of two pups born to a small female stray. She had appeared one day when I was about six or seven years old. She stayed and a few weeks later a male dog, white with large irregular reddish-brown spots arrived. He was aloof and did not seem especially friendly. He stayed for a few weeks and then simply vanished as quietly as he had arrived.

I discovered the two puppies while searching for eggs after hearing one of our hens cackling in one of the sheds. I was unable to locate the nest initially, but was able to move some bales of hay and create a path to the back part of the shed. There I found the hen's nest and heard some sort of whimpering. Eventually, I was able to move closer to the source and spotted the two small puppies! How the mother found that hiding place and how she could get in and out was puzzling. It was several days before the puppies could be seen on a regular basis.

Buster was a robust puppy, a duplicate of his sire, while Ricky was clearly the smaller of the two. We were excited...we had puppies! Actually, my younger sister, Ellen, and I were excited about the puppies; the remainder of our family was neutral at best. We had just assumed that the puppies belonged to us. Their mother took care of them, trained them and always seemed to resent our interference. She would regularly take both pups away from the house in an apparent attempt to prevent us from playing with them. She was simply doing what she needed to do which was something that we could not comprehend.

When the pups were approximately ten weeks old, she took them across the highway and into a large field. Several minutes later I heard the driver of a large truck frantically blowing the horn; only Buster and his mother returned, running as fast as they could. There was no doubt about what had happened to Ricky.

Buster's mother disappeared one day before he was even half-grown. Apparently, she simply left and Buster either chose to stay or she just discouraged him from accompanying her. It did not matter anyway, Buster was a survivor. And he had us to care for him. We tried to teach him some tricks, but we lacked the knowledge, expertise and patience to accomplish anything much more than to impart the ability to shake hands.

Buster hated rats and snakes, having been bitten by both. Although from hunting stock (at least on one side), he showed no real talent for hunting. Of course, he had no training, either. Buster was simply a farm dog and companion. He was brave if you were at his side when it was dark and the red wolves came up to steal chickens, but without you nearby he would guard the back door of the house, hoping that those wolves were only after the chickens! Buster was always there when I went outside and remained with me until I returned.

He was an outside dog; he was never allowed in the house except during one terrible thunderstorm when my mother relented and gave permission to let him enter the house. Although happy to be inside, he was not comfortable in the house and eagerly returned outside when the storm subsided. Ellen and I would sneak him into the house at other times, but the waxed hardwood floors terrified him if he attempted to move quickly.

Buster patrolled the barbed wire fences for those

errant cattle that poked their heads between the strands of wire in search of the taller, greener grass on the proverbial other side of the fence. Since the pasture area virtually encircled the house except for the long driveway, he usually observed his self-imposed area of responsibility from the yard. He would stalk his target with great stealth followed by a short sprint and deliver a quick nip to the nose which usually did the trick.

He also did his very best to help eradicate the rat population that lived in and around the barn and other outbuildings. Of course he usually needed some human assistance to move various objects and expose the nests and hiding places. I once watched him kill nine rats that scurried nine different directions when their hiding place was overturned; he was quick, methodical and very efficient. As a pup, he had been bitten by a large rat that probably did not understand that the pup was just curious and not a threat. Buster developed an incredible hatred of rats probably due to that incident.

Buster also dispatched snakes of any variety, including at least one water moccasin that managed to bite him in the process. His face swelled tremendously, but he suffered no other ill effects. We did not take him to the veterinarian since it was apparently not a life-threatening situation and he was, after all, just a farm dog.

Buster also provided companionship to my younger sister and me. We had no nearby neighbors with children our age, so we were often forced to invent our own entertainment. That poor dog suffered some incredible indignities at our hands as we invented all sorts of roles for him. While he tolerated our unusual actions, he clearly preferred to just do those things that dogs do best. He was a star at any game involving a chase. We spent countless hours attempting to catch him as he carried some small object and stayed just out of our reach. He was fast and could change directions so easily that we never caught him until he allowed it.

Buster provided additional entertainment by taunting some of our cows that had small calves. These were mostly Brahman cows which had reputations for fiercely protecting their offspring. Buster's mere presence was enough to trigger a chase. He easily avoided the cows and seemed to thoroughly enjoy this exciting sport. He was certainly not a threat to the calves and thus was never discouraged from this game. On rare occasions he failed to notice a second cow that had joined the melee and paid the price, but without real injury. At other times he was able to grab the tail of one of the cows causing her to spin around in an attempt to get him. Buster would become airborne as the frantic cow spun even faster in order to catch him. He would eventually either lose his grip or the cow would stop; in either case, the angry and disoriented cow would try to chase the dizzy dog as he wobbled his way to safety.

Buster also provided some serious assistance. We had a bout with a nighttime prowler for several years and Buster always announced his arrival. The prowler tried to win his friendship by feeding him, yet Buster always let us know that an intruder was in the area. We were not able to catch the prowler, but always found evidence of his presence. Buster, our loyal guardian, was always there, keeping watch.

As I grew older, I had less time to devote to my four-legged friend. School and sports took up more of my time and it was easy to postpone a romp with full intentions of making it up to him on the weekends. The weekends often went by without that special time together, but I certainly had not abandoned him.

He disappeared for a couple of days while I was in high school and returned one morning horribly mauled by some unknown animal. The extent of his injuries is still vivid and we all knew that he would probably not survive the trip to the vet. It is remarkable that he was even able to reach home.

I was given the task of putting him down. Pistol in hand, I walked to "the place" while Buster plodded along with me. The lump in my throat made speech impossible. Tears were flowing when we stopped and he looked up at me with his one remaining eye. Then he turned his head away as if he knew what was about to happen. Shaking and feeling like I had somehow betrayed him, I ended his suffering. I promised myself that I would never again become attached to a dog.

I had a lot of time to remember the many instances when I failed to spend a few hours or even a few minutes with Buster. There was a lot of guilt because I had never really had a good excuse.

We acquired another dog soon thereafter, but it was just not the same. I never made a real attempt to make him part of my life.

****

Over the years we acquired various cats, dogs, rats, rabbits, fish and hamsters as pets for our two daughters and some just lasted longer than others. For me there was never that special bond that I remember having had with Buster. They were pets, just transient animals in our lives. My last tour of duty in the Navy was at Naval Air Station Memphis, Tennessee where we rented a farmhouse and acquired a young male Weimaraner as part of the deal. That experience sowed the seeds of affection for this very special breed. I could not foresee where this might lead...he was, after all, just a dog.

Chapter 2

Spunky

It really doesn't seem that long ago and yet the calendar tells me otherwise. It was the summer of 1984 and I had just transferred from Hawaii to Memphis, Tennessee. My pilot skills were not required for that next tour of duty and I expected some semblance of a "normal" five-day workweek. I had grown up on a farm and something inside kept urging me to go there again. Everything was better back then or at least it seemed that way. I had actually looked forward to the hard work that would certainly ensue.

With my wife and youngest daughter, Donna, assisting in the project, we began a search for a temporary home. Donna was quick to remind me that I had promised her a place where she could raise a horse. She had worked at the riding stables at Naval Air Station Barbers Point in Hawaii and had become an accomplished rider with a special love for horses. I had forgotten about the promise, but on our second day in Tennessee she located a mare and young colt for sale. Thus our search for a house focused on a rental with a few acres of land and a small barn or stable.

Luckily, while I was transferring to my new duty station, another individual was transferring out and he needed to rent out his mini-farm. We discussed all of the particulars and everything that we needed was included in the rental; it seemed just too good to be true. He and his family would be departing soon and timing could not have been any better. We reached an agreement that solved both of our problems.

He mentioned that he had two Weimaraners, but would only be taking one with him. We were welcome to take the available dog or he would find a home for it...he was not concerned either way since this particular dog was not on a par with the other. It appeared to be an easy decision on his part. I suppose that I considered the possibility that the dog might be put to sleep if no one wanted him.

I told him that I would take the dog while everything inside told me (actually screamed) that it would be a big mistake. A few weeks later it was time to leave our temporary lodging and move into the rental. Our furniture and other personal goods had arrived and the other family had begun the process of moving to their new duty station.

On moving day we were introduced to "Sputnik," a sleek young male Weimaraner. "That name's gotta go," I remember thinking. Sputnik was on a run set up between two trees. We visited with the other family for a few minutes and wished them well as they departed. After the other family had been gone for several minutes, I released Sputnik and let him run around for a minute and then told him to "come!" He ran straight to me, sat and looked me squarely in the eyes. That was it, I knew that I had made the right choice. I don't really know what made me so certain that this dog was anything special, but there was absolutely no concern that he would be a problem. He was the lightest color of gray that Weimaraners come in although I did not know that at the time. His eyes were a haunting golden color that never failed to generate comments from those who saw him.

We played for a few minutes and I reluctantly hooked him up to the run again since moving in was our main priority and we could not take the time to make certain that he did not stray. During those hectic hours we discussed various names and decided that the new name should sound similar to his present name. The best name that we could come up with was "Spunky" and it turned out to be a perfect description; he responded to it immediately. Within two days he was off the run and was always waiting at the back door and ready for any adventure.

Spunky would accompany me anywhere and his only rule was that he must arrive first. There were cats that also came with the farm and Spunky paid no attention to them at all. One morning, though, the mother cat was acting strangely in a grassy part of the yard not far from her kittens. I cautiously approached the cat with Spunky out in front as usual. There was a large rat snake moving toward the kittens. Though the mother cat placed herself between the snake and her hiding place, the snake moved relentlessly toward the kittens. Spunky spotted the snake and at some point decided that it was some sort of threat. It was obvious that he had never encountered a snake before and was extremely surprised when it struck at him. Since it was not a poisonous snake, I allowed him to continue. After a few clumsy attempts, he grabbed the snake and quickly dispatched it. He shook it numerous times, dropped it and repeated the process over and over again. I never saw another snake anywhere on the property after that.

Weeks went by and during one of our forays into the wooded section of the property, I noticed that he was winded by only a small amount of exertion. Later I detected a pronounced wheezing and coughing and soon we were on our way to the veterinarian. A blood test revealed the presence of heartworms; the vet stated that his heart was literally being impaired by their size and quantity. The vet then pointed out a dissected canine heart on display which was filled with heartworms. That was all it took...time for a major decision: put Spunky down or go through the risky heartworm treatment.

The treatments consisted of killing the heartworms at a slow rate so that his body could absorb them and hope that they would not break loose and kill him. We opted for the treatment and took him home with strict instructions to keep him calm and inactive. We kept him in a horse stall in the barn for a few days hoping to limit his movement. He hated the separation from the family and great care was necessary to prevent him from slipping out of the stall when the door was opened. He was able to escape once and went for a romp despite our attempts to call him to us. I expected him to collapse at any moment and tried walking toward him in the hope that he would allow me to grab his collar. No such luck...he was free and intended to stay that way. Chasing him was out of the question.

Eventually he returned and allowed me to capture him; he seemed fine. We watched him closely for several hours, expecting the worst, but observed no ill effects. Perhaps we were extremely lucky or maybe the vet was just overly cautious. Ultimately, the treatment was successful and soon he was good as new and on heartworm medication. I had never even heard of heartworms before. Furthermore, I do not remember a single instance in my childhood when we took a dog to the vet because dogs were "just dogs" and their status was not high enough to warrant the expense. I do not mean to imply that this was cruel or neglectful, but our dogs just never suffered serious injuries...except for that final episode with Buster.

Months later Spunky failed to greet me at the back door. When he did finally appear, he was limping and I noticed a small entrance and exit wound in one leg...he had been shot! The vet took care of the wound and found a SECOND wound only this one was completely healed and the bullet was still there! He explained that since the bullet was not creating a problem he preferred not to remove it. His next statement was a complete surprise. "These are both .22 caliber wounds...most people around here use a shotgun for dogs." That was a shock. It was time for one more decision: would neutering stop the roaming? "Maybe." And so Spunky lost his previous social status and his solo roaming essentially ceased over the next few weeks. You might ask why he was allowed to run loose and I would have explained that he was a farm dog and was thoroughly versed in the art of avoiding cars and trucks on those Tennessee back roads. And who would have thought that anyone would shoot such a handsome dog!

Our oldest daughter, Debbie, came to Tennessee for the Christmas holidays and was a welcome addition. Although not initially thrilled by the country lifestyle, she enjoyed the chance to experience the slower pace and sample some of the simpler pleasures of farm life. It was great to see both daughters having fun more as equals than as competitors.

As the New Year approached, a special treat in the form of fireworks awaited the family and several inches of snow made the entire place resemble a picture postcard scene. During the height of the New Years Eve Fireworks Extravaganza, I relocated one skyrocket to a position where it would be crossing our field of view at a better angle. The launching trajectory would take it through an open area devoid of tree branches and the view was certain to be spectacular. It was, though not as planned.

The skyrocket somehow went up into the tree branches, ricocheted, turned around and blasted right into Spunky's well-insulated doghouse! Had it been planned, it would have been on a par with a lunar launch by NASA! This was followed by the exit of The World's Fastest Weimaraner! Seconds later, a strange light shown from the doghouse entrance as the starburst ignited and a few tracers spewed from the door. Spunky never used that doghouse again and there were no more fireworks extravaganzas. (Mental note: Weimaraners do not like fireworks...especially up close!)

A few months later we were able to buy a house on 10 acres of land and eagerly moved in. Spunky loved the open areas and was Donna's companion when she rode her horse. He had begun to assume the role of protector even though I had never even heard him growl. On one occasion Donna was sunbathing in the backyard and Spunky was sleeping perhaps twenty feet away. She chose this time to sit up, stretch and yawn. That yawn included a sound resembling a scream and what happened next was one of the most impressive sights I have ever seen.

Spunky went from sound asleep at the carport to her side in a split second! More importantly, he was alert, hair-on-end, dancing around and ready to defend her from whatever the danger was. He appeared to be twice his normal size and even I was not inclined to approach him. What a magnificent specimen! I gained a profound respect and admiration for this wonderful dog who "didn't measure up." Up until that point I had not considered Spunky to be a threat to anyone or anything except snakes.

Spunky was not our only dog. We also had acquired a Doberman named "Duke" and a German Shepherd mix named "Shadow." Duke was not allowed to run loose due to the reputation of the breed as perceived by the neighbors. Shadow was replaced by a Beagle (who was NOT named Snoopy). One day the Beagle brought us a baby mourning dove that was slightly injured but alive. I took the bird and began caring for it as best I could. A few minutes later the beagle presented me with a second mourning dove with no injuries whatsoever. Try as I might, I could only coax the injured bird to eat the baby chick food that I presented to them. The survivor grew rapidly and when fully feathered was absolutely gorgeous. We began teaching it to fly in the safety of our screened porch. We also sprinkled its food on the floor so that it was forced to search for it. Soon we would be releasing the beautiful bird.

We had one very important rule: make certain that the dove was in its cage before allowing the dogs to enter the screened porch. One evening while the dove was loose, I entered the screened porch and was greeted by Spunky with the lifeless dove in his mouth. He was so proud and placed the dove in my outstretched hand with great care. I was angry about the deed and yet aware of Spunky's instincts and told him what a good boy he was. The culprit and her accomplice were so saddened by the event that nothing further was ever said. I had not even considered Spunky to be a bird dog since I was unaware of any exposure to hunting. I suppose that even without training, some dogs simply carry out those actions that are ingrained.

On another occasion, I was moving one of our steers from one pen to another using a long rope. This steer did not lead well (actually not at all) and progress was slow. At one point he balked and refused to move. It was soon obvious that I could not pull him to the pen. I walked up to him, slapped him on the hip and he took off! His five hundred-pound weight advantage was going to cause me some major problems, so I ran along with him hoping to lessen the shock and perhaps turn him when he reached the end of the rope. It worked! I was even gaining and pulling in some of the rope while coming up alongside as he slowed. Since he was going in the right direction, why mess with a good thing. Without warning, a gray missile named Spunky came to my "rescue" and began growling and snapping at the steer's legs so that I could escape.

This breathed new life into the steer and my wife and daughter began cheering as the game elevated to new heights! I was out of breath and could not even yell at Spunky to stop. Besides, I had no word or phrase to tell Spunky to leave the steer alone; I mean that's not something we had ever worked on! I tried yelling for somebody to call Spunky, but the show was so hilarious that their continuous cheering and laughter drowned out my weak calls for help. They were completely unaware that I was in serious trouble. In my attempt to pull the rope in, some of the rope had wrapped around parts of my anatomy, of which I am quite fond and this provided me with sufficient motivation to continue running at the same speed as the steer!

Spunky, however, was fresh and unburdened and could keep this up for a long time. My only hope was the steer. Have you ever tried talking to a crazed animal when you can't even get enough air to breathe? I maintained that delicate balance of letting the steer pull me while I did all I could to keep from falling and ultimately we all came to a stop. Immediately a stupid little voice inside of me spoke out loud to Spunky and said "Good boy!" It could not have been my voice since I was thinking other things and none were complimentary.

Spunky taught me many things, but I never explored the possibilities that existed with this wonderful dog. He had the ability to learn quickly yet I never seized the opportunity to push his limits. I never knew anything about his heritage, but he had a special, regal air about him. He loved to play rough yet was never a danger to anyone. He was Donna's protector and accompanied her and her horse on their many rides around the area. One of my favorite memories is a brisk winter morning and Spunky curled up with the other dogs with a cat peacefully sleeping on his back.

When it was time to move on, Spunky remained with the new owners of our house; it was not possible to take him with us. I've thought about him many times since then and always considered him far more than "just a dog." Those four years with Spunky had been really great, but I had never let him "get" to me; I was determined to keep that promise from years before.

Chapter 3

The Search for a Puppy

Fast forward to late 1995. There had been many changes in my life since leaving Tennessee. I retired from the Navy, divorced, re-married and was living in Plymouth, Massachusetts with my wife, Bobbie, step-son, Michael plus two cats, Rocky and Charlotte. The two cats had been Bobbie's pets for many years and they had begun to show the effects of aging. Kidney, joint and bladder problems had become acute and their quality of life had deteriorated dramatically. We (actually Bobbie) finally made the decision to have them put to sleep, which had been the veterinarian's recommendation some time earlier. I was working at Pilgrim Nuclear Power Station in Security and was able to take the cats to the vet after my shift ended. Bobbie had asked me to just greet her one day at the door when she returned from work and simply tell her that Rocky and Charlotte had gone to "kitty heaven." She said she would cry and then go on with her life. I did; she did and she did.

Her pets of more than fifteen years had put some restrictions on our lives, mostly in the form of travel. Michael's work schedule often made it virtually impossible for Bobbie and me to go places due to the extra care required for the two cats. We suddenly had the freedom to travel without need for extensive care arrangements for the two cats and we were able to go places previously denied to us. This was a big help in alleviating Bobbie's sense of loss of the two pets. We used our newly found independence to visit many of the attractions in the area and thoroughly enjoyed ourselves. Even so, there was just something missing. Both cats had always made their presence known in the evenings, just swinging by and reminding us that they were there, but never making any real demands. Let's face it, they were independent and aloof. That had been part of our routine and we secretly missed it. It only took six months until we both finally acknowledged that we needed to replace the cats.

A huge tomcat had appeared at the back door during the previous winter much to the chagrin of Rocky and Charlotte. We had fed him since there was considerable snow on the ground and he wore no collar. He was somewhat thin, but not emaciated. We felt sorry for him and hoped that he would move on and find his way home. Due to his size and since he was a stranger, we chose not to attempt to capture him. He became a regular visitor and gradually allowed us to pet him. He exhibited good manners and never scratched or bit anyone.

Without Rocky and Charlotte we were able to grant him more attention and the frequency of his visits continually increased. We even took him to a veterinarian to have him checked and the vet marveled at his size.

A few days later the vet called to inform us that the cat had feline HIV. He was the picture of health and it was difficult to comprehend that anything could be wrong with that animal. We allowed him into the house and he adapted quickly. A few days later, during a visit, he made the mistake of "marking his territory" in the house and was banished forever from the inside. Nevertheless he still visited us daily. Perhaps it was just lack of inspiration, but we named him simply "Big Kitty." Even his considerable presence was not enough to fill the pet void. We needed something more.

We considered getting a dog since Bobbie had owned one before and I was certainly agreeable to the extra responsibility involved. Her first question was, "What breed?" This became the big issue. What breed would fit our lifestyle? Neither of us had a large personal database of breeds from which to draw. We purchased various dog magazines and suddenly began noticing every dog on a leash or running on the beach. Where did all of these dogs come from? I doubt that the numbers increased, we just were paying more attention. We spoke to their owners and **every** dog was the best dog that they had ever owned. No problems and no bad habits...so much for unbiased opinions! We spent hours at pet stores looking at puppies.

As you probably know, puppies sell themselves on the spot and many people take home that cute little puppy without doing their research. Parents may purchase a puppy for their children and despite the earlier promises, the parents end up taking care of the dog. Additionally, that little puppy usually changes into something much larger and far more demanding than anyone had ever envisioned. The expense involved is always more than expected and obedience training is not always accomplished. The lovable little puppy may become an annoyance or may possibly begin to exhibit aggressive tendencies. It may even become unmanageable and ultimately end up at the local animal shelter. This would NOT be the case with our dog...we would do this the right way!

We eliminated the "giant" dogs easily; they were just too large and we wanted a dog that could be comfortable in our small home. I mentioned to Bobbie that the dog would be primarily an outside animal and she smiled with that expression that really means, "Are you stupid?" I had not even considered the possibility of a dog living in the house. Winters were cold, but insulated doghouses are available and temporary house access during extreme weather would certainly be okay. Besides, that was really a consideration for a later date.

We eliminated the toy breeds in much the same manner, but it wasn't so much their size as it was their bark. Even the "large" breeds were removed from our choices since we had limited space. Next we eliminated those dogs with coats requiring what we perceived as excessive care; the continuous brushing requirements and shedding problems just were not acceptable to us. This still left dozens of breeds. We then sought to avoid any breed known for loud, aggressive or nervous tendencies. Thus bit by bit we were moving toward our vision of the ideal dog.

Out of the blue I picked up a magazine and was thumbing through the pages when I encountered the photo of an absolutely beautiful Vizsla. The color and shine of the coat were impressive; the look and the expression were elegant. I showed the photo to Bobbie and she was equally impressed. Perhaps our search was over. At some point I mentioned the similarity to a Weimaraner and that added a little more confusion. So we bounced back and forth trying to decide which breed to choose. The Vizsla had the edge due to its size. Yet the slightly larger Weimaraner had those remarkable eyes and my experiences with Spunky proved to be a powerful influence on me while Bobbie remained neutral. We persisted with our efforts on behalf of the Vizsla and due to some unusual circumstances saw only Vizslas with what we considered to be less than perfect heads. That was not the governing factor, but it did play a major role. Would our puppy grow up to have a head similar to the one we saw in the photo or would it resemble the ones we had most recently seen? Keep in mind that we were anxious to find the perfect breed and the perfect puppy. Oh, and it could not be a male because males are "not always discreet." That may explain why no professional male athletes are allowed to live at our house.

Bobbie searched for Weimaraner breeders in our area and eventually located one not too far away. She visited the breeder at her workplace and came home with some good news and some bad news. The good news was that she spent several minutes chatting with the breeder before noticing a motionless Weimaraner standing just a few feet away with its front feet on a counter. She thought it was a statue. She was introduced to the dog and was amazed at the beauty and demeanor of this silent, well-mannered animal. That dog actually made the decision for her. The bad news: the breeder would not sell a puppy to us since our yard was not fenced.

Our intent was to purchase and install one of the "invisible fences." It did not matter...no deal. Invisible fences would keep the puppy IN, but would not keep other dogs OUT. Bobbie relayed this information to me and I was at a loss to understand the breeder's rationale. I suppose that I really DID understand, but I thought it would be OUR problem not hers. Okay, there were other breeders.

Finding other breeders turned out to be a major challenge. I had never seen an ad for Weimaraner puppies in a newspaper or posted on a supermarket bulletin board. We could find nothing in the yellow pages (Did you know that PETS is located right behind PESTS...is this significant?). Those breeders that had ads in the various dog magazines were located too far away. Keep in mind that to us the term *breeder* meant someone (by then ANYONE) who had Weimaraners and would sell one to us. At this same time we were unable to locate one in a pet store. We did not know that pet store puppies usually came from "puppy mills" and were confused when pet store personnel could not answer exactly where the puppies came from. Invariably, they were all "subject to registration" and both the sire and dam were ALWAYS champions. Once we were even told that the puppy was a champion because both PARENTS were champions! We did not know anything about dog shows, but we did know that champion status is not bestowed on a puppy due to the status of the sire and dam.

We were finally able to locate a breeder in Monson, Massachusetts. Sue Thomas of Camelot Kennels seemed very nice over the phone and invited us out to the kennel to see some of her Weimaraners. We made the two-hour drive to the kennel and fell in love with all of the puppies and were impressed with every adult dog that we saw. We explained that we wanted a "pet quality" female puppy rather than a "show dog." We did not care if she were show quality, we simply had no intention of showing her. And of course we would have her spayed.

We were not prepared for the grilling that followed. After explaining that "pet quality" puppies were not common, Sue discussed how our lifestyle and our home were a major concern to her. The buyer had to meet HER standards before she would sell. Would the dog be left alone? Was the yard fenced? Would we take the time to properly care for the dog? Why did we want a female instead of a male? The questions seemed endless and she concluded with the statement that all of her puppies were already spoken for. So after putting us through all of that, there were no available puppies? We were crushed. Thus we were placed on a list with four people ahead of us. The biggest surprise was that her puppies were sold at a price comparable to those at the pet store. She invited us to an upcoming dog show where we could see several of her dogs in the ring and we departed the kennel trying to understand why breeders were so fussy and pet store personnel were so uninformed and pushy.

Periodically we called the kennel to learn where we stood on the list but never seemed to move up. We even made a special trip to the kennel just to see the puppies and to see where we were on the list...hoping that our mere presence would spark some action. Nothing. Two months went by and we had only moved up to second on the list. We knew that at least two litters had arrived during that time and my mathematical expertise told me that we should have been nearing the top of the list by that time. We had taken her up on the dog show offer and had seen numerous Weimaraners and even re-visited the Vizsla idea since there were a few of them there also. Sue could not have any doubts as to our sincerity. Our morale was falling and we were becoming desperate. We considered other breeders, but had failed to talk to any at the dog show. At least Sue had made an effort and that was all we had.

We were still in the "pet quality" mode and in early July (1996) I called Sue for an update. She stated that she had this fear of selling a puppy and seeing it months later as a potential national champion except that the dog had been spayed/neutered by the owners. Sue then asked if we would consider co-ownership. She explained the basic concept and requirements which I scribbled down hastily without paying complete attention to everything she said. Then she dropped the bombshell: she had a puppy for us if we were willing to go the co-ownership route! After letting her words sink in for a few seconds, she asked if we were interested. I was desperate! I agreed immediately, got her mailing address and called Bobbie with the good news. Co-ownership was not what we had intended, but we would soon have our puppy! We mailed our deposit that afternoon. Bobbie had already picked her name: Hilde.

Chapter 4

The Perfect Puppy

We brought Hilde home on a Saturday two weeks later and our lives changed forever. We had never seen such a beautiful puppy! Ten weeks old, her eyes were still showing some blue but were becoming more of an amber color. The drive home seemed to take forever even though we talked to her and brought her out of her small crate. She informed us that she had to "go" before we had completed the trip and it seemed as if housebreaking would be very easy.

Once we arrived home we took her out into the backyard and let her become familiar with her new surroundings. I had built a temporary pen while waiting on the installation of a chain link fence. This gave her the necessary space to run and provided us with an acceptable level of security. We were in awe over the new arrival. Of course she spent the remainder of that first day with us hovering over her and she loved the attention. She took a brief nap which resulted in the two of us constantly checking to see if she was awake.

As darkness approached, we brought her into the house and played with her until she fell asleep. It was so difficult to let her sleep, but we did and just watched her. We smiled a lot. Sue had sent us home with a stack of papers which covered our co-ownership agreement plus medical and other information. She also provided the serum ingredients for Hilde's inoculation protocol and worming medications for us to administer. Additionally, there was the American Kennel Club (AKC) registration form and we completed our portion, adding her AKC name: Camelot's Mathilde. Sue required that the kennel name be part of the AKC name. We accomplished the paperwork while Hilde napped.

That first night Hilde cried after being placed into her crate. We moved her into our bedroom so she wouldn't keep all of us awake. She whimpered a little and soon went to sleep on my briefly worn tee shirt without any further protest. Of course I let her out once so that she could empty her bladder and she immediately went back to sleep. Every night she improved. If it was necessary to leave her unattended, she was either restricted to the kitchen or the backyard. Housebreaking was easy...just one or two accidents and then no further problems. We were ecstatic! There was no doubt that we had the perfect puppy.

During the normal workweek, I was able to come home at lunchtime to check on her and usually had time to play briefly with her. This arrangement was working very well and there was no indication of separation anxiety. Of course when Bobbie and I both returned home at the end of the workday, we smothered Hilde with attention. The days were still long enough that we could play with her for several hours before the sun went down. We cooked outside as much as possible just so we could keep her in sight.

I love those juice bars that come on a stick and always managed to have a little left for Hilde. She seemed to think that those little treats were so very special. Her energy level was incredibly high and it was tiring just to watch her play. She eventually met Big Kitty who was approximately her size and other than the initial mild curiosity, they never had any incidents...at least not then. Obviously, she was the perfect puppy.

We anticipated visits from grandchildren, neighbors, nieces and nephews. It was only natural to assume that sooner or later one of the children would touch Hilde at the wrong time. Would Hilde bite? We found a list of things that might cause a dog to bite and began to teach Hilde to accept them. We petted her while she ate. We took her food dish away. We even took food out of her mouth. Basically we taught her to accept everything that the list warned about. She grew up with these restrictions and accepted them. We never thought much about it after that, but then what would you expect from the perfect puppy?

Hilde had two speeds: wide open and sound asleep. She would play until she collapsed. When called, she ran at top speed but apparently nature does not instill in all puppies the simple concept of stopping. Therefore, she would crash into you to stop and at first it was cute, but she GREW! Rough play with Hilde was tough; my hands and arms always showed the effects of her sharp teeth. Canine aggression was not on our minds; we did not know that we were encouraging some potentially dangerous actions. And photos...we took photos! We had the puppy books, the toys and of course the cute leash and collar combo. She was progressing well on the leash and when we said, "come" she CAME! We were thrilled.

During one of my lunch hour checks on her, I was amazed to see a large male swan outside the fence with Hilde inside, front leg raised in an impressive point. It was so ludicrous, but a precursor of the behavior that would be demonstrated on a regular basis. When I returned with the camera, the swan was gone and Hilde was looking for more game to tame. The swan never returned. Was she good or what! That was just another indication that she was the perfect puppy.

By the book (actually several books) I taught her "sit," "down," "stay" and "come." Actually, she taught herself to sit; we just said the word. We also taught her to "go" on command. That turned out to be a blessing. On another of those lunchtime visits I taught her SIT, DOWN, STAY and COME by hand signal and she had it down pat in fifteen minutes. When I came home from work she again followed the hand signals perfectly.

Upon Bobbie's return from work, I showed her the hand signals and told her to try it. She took Hilde to the far side of the yard and gave the signal to sit, followed by "down" and then "stay." She turned her back and walked to the opposite side of the yard and was amazed to see Hilde exactly as she had left her. Bobbie knelt down, hesitated and then gave her the "come" signal and Hilde streaked to her (Oh yeah, gotta teach her to stop!). Picking herself up, Bobbie expressed her amazement. Certainly we must have gotten the perfect puppy.

We bought Hilde some rawhide chew items and soon she developed an appetite for our leather shoes. Another lesson learned. We bought some *bitter apple* and sprayed it all over the forbidden items, but she didn't care...she chewed them anyway! We used expandable wooden gates to keep her confined to the kitchen and she chewed off ONLY the one piece of wood with a different color; once that was accomplished, she felt no further need to chew the gates. She never chewed any wooden furniture. She did chew part of the skirt on our sofa (we needed a new sofa anyway). We splurged on a very nice (expensive) crate cushion for our perfect puppy...she ate it! We had done an excellent job of puppy-proofing the house especially in the area of electrical wiring. On one occasion we returned home to find the portable kitchen telephone wiring chewed and the phone inoperable (we needed a new phone anyway). That was the only incident with wiring. It was amazing how Hilde knew which items in our house needed replacing! Maybe that's how we knew she was the perfect puppy.

Canvas toys with plastic squeakers inside were her favorite toys and that remains true even today. However, there was a certain type of canvas kitty that she absolutely adored. She would quickly remove the ears and all other items which helped identify it as a kitty. As a family joke, when the kitty was ready for retirement, we would ship it to Bobbie's parents down in Florida. Imagine our surprise on our first visit to Florida (after acquiring Hilde) to find all of those sad looking kitties lined up waiting for us! When Hilde removed the first squeaker from the toy, we were concerned that it might become lodged in her throat. When we mentioned that possibility to Michael he recommended that she sleep in another room if the whistling bothered us! He was kidding...I think.

There was another item of concern. Bobbie and I swore that we would not use the terms "mommy" and "daddy" when referring to ourselves in front of Hilde. That lasted only a week or two. Before you roll your eyes and shake your head, remember that the alternative was to be on a first name basis and I found that to be even more ludicrous. Keep in mind that we normally use those terms in the privacy of our own home due to the funny stares that we receive in public. And for what it's worth, we thought it was somewhat perverse until we started doing it. Ah, the sacrifices for the perfect puppy!

There were restrictions placed on our perfect puppy. "Hilde will never be allowed on the furniture." That one probably lasted three weeks at the most. How could you refuse that little charmer when all she wanted was to be close to you? All three of us were guilty of breaking that rule and Hilde began to take it for granted. It was just too hard to reverse the trend and it was several months before we admitted that we had ALL been letting her up on the furniture. We DID draw the line at begging for food at the table...begging was NOT tolerated. We were exceptionally strict about giving her table scraps except vegetables and fruits. Hilde was never a problem eater and was (and is) very food efficient.

The breeder established Hilde's initial dietary preferences; we continued with the same brand of dry dog food even though it was not sold everywhere. Thus we were forced to visit pet stores. Pet stores have evolved into places of awe and excitement and dogs probably regard them the same way. Most even encourage you to bring your leashed dog into the store. That was a real eye opener! Hilde in a pet store is much like me in a large discount hardware store...time stands still and there is SO MUCH to see. I think we normally spend more money at the pet store, though.

On her first visit, Hilde checked out everything that she would like to eat or chew specialty foods, cookies, various rawhide items, treats, beef hooves and bones.

The second visit included all of the previous items and added birds, rabbits and the sleek ferrets. It was not a good idea to hold the leash lightly if you were in an area where the "goodies" moved. When Hilde's motivation was derived from a live, moving target, her strength and drive were a sight to behold! Other customers quickly gave us a wide berth. The cashiers ALWAYS took our money but NEVER asked us to come back; perhaps they were unaware that Hilde was the perfect puppy.

Pet stores also provide other services including photographers who specialize in pets. Of course we had hundreds of photos by this time and we really did not need a portrait of Hilde. Well, I didn't think we needed one, but one of those cashiers (probably on commission and one of the same ones who never asked us to come back) told us what a beautiful dog Hilde was. She then pointed at a display which a photographer had set up near the exit. The basic pitch was that we would really be low-life scum if we failed to sign up for a portrait. We caved. Eighty dollars later we had a really great photo on mock canvas with a massive wooden frame. Soon it was on the wall over the fireplace mantle. It had THE exalted location in our house. No spouse, child or relative ever received such treatment. But then, Hilde was the perfect puppy.

We were surprised one morning by Hilde sneezing constantly. Could it be allergies? Do dogs get colds? After perhaps ten sneezes, I checked her nose and noticed something in one of her nostrils. I was unable to grasp it and grabbed some tweezers. I extracted a cluster of pine needles! The cluster consisted of three pine needles that had somehow entered the nostril with the points entering first. Leave it to Hilde to pull that off!

Reading through the various puppy books we had found that most were in agreement when it came to training and rewards. The biggest problem was disciplining the dog. Hilde already knew the meaning of "no" and we usually had no problem in that regard. We were careful not to use her name followed by "No!" I remember hearing or reading that the sound of her name was automatically a "good" or "happy" sound to her which must not be followed by the "No!" to avoid confusion. Why should we be concerned...we had the perfect puppy.

There were times, though, when we needed to punish her, but striking Hilde was never an option. One article that we found stressed the canine "pack" structure. Basically there is one "pack leader" and the dog must be inferior to all human members of his/her "pack." WEIMARANER WAYS proved to be our best source of information with a photo showing a mother dog disciplining her puppy. The basic idea is to put the puppy on its back or side and hold it motionless until the dog relaxes or submits. We also knew that a deep voice scolding the puppy was another method.

Once, Hilde committed some act of defiance and I disciplined her using both the physical and the verbal actions. As soon as she submitted, I gave her one last shake and walked away. After a minute or so I set up the same situation as before and she committed the same act of defiance. Justice was swift and this time I was slower to walk away. That stopped the defiance and it was many weeks before the need for punishment reoccurred. Soon just a stare or a warning in a low voice was all that was required. I received a lot of grief from Bobbie and Michael on that style of punishment until they tried it. What a difference when you do things the way the puppy understands! Growling also works, but always look around for the presence of other people before you do it!

Hilde always tried to make up and regain her pre-discipline status. She would whine, cry and use some of her many heart-melting expressions and it was extremely difficult not to relent too soon. What a little con artist, but then she was the perfect puppy!

Hilde was becoming a bigger part of our lives and every day brought change. We carefully recorded her weight on a weekly basis. She quickly learned to sit on the bathroom scales which was greatly appreciated as she gained weight; it was becoming increasingly difficult to hold her in my arms and read the scales. Of course, then we had to subtract my weight from the total.

We searched for a new veterinarian, one who was familiar with Weimaraners. They are not the most popular breed and thus it took some time to locate a vet. We found one who had been recommended by several friends and decided to check him out. During the office visit I asked him how large we could expect Hilde to grow, knowing that the answer was approximately sixty or seventy pounds. He said, "Up to one hundred twenty pounds." He stayed with that figure when I challenged it. He also refused to follow the inoculation protocol provided by our breeder, dismissing it as "just hype" concerning the breed. It was already time to look for a new vet! We ended up back at our old vet, Dr. Newman. Oh well, he was closer anyway. We would do what was necessary and take no chances involving the perfect puppy.

About this same time Hilde expressed a strong desire to stand with two front feet on the kitchen counters. This was a serious offense and was always met with a resounding "No!" She also used the same posture to look through the back door window, but that was not a problem from our point of view. When caught in the act Hilde's solution was to drop one paw and tilt her head backwards until it was upside-down. The first time I saw that I laughed out loud. That did it...that became her special thing and we allowed it. If she forgot and placed both front feet on the counter or back door, the situation could be corrected by just saying her name. She would immediately drop one foot and then turn her head upside-down! She would not put the other foot back up. The counter received additional cleaning and a few months later she stopped putting her paws there. We had a small step stool in the kitchen...that is where she began placing her front feet. She would then raise her head as high as possible and assume a haughty yet regal pose. That was an excellent compromise and she had chosen to do that because she was the perfect puppy.

****

On one of our earlier visits to the local plant nursery, we had spotted an absolutely perfect "rose tree" and an equally impressive miniature rose plant. These had been purchased and carefully nurtured in the back yard. The thorns would prevent Hilde from destroying them and their portable nature would allow us to move them into the cellar for the upcoming winter. Of course Hilde uprooted the miniature rose and basically ate it...suffering no ill effects whatsoever. With that success, she moved on to bigger and better things: the rose tree. She uprooted it by digging in the container and pulling it out. Luckily this occurred just prior to my arrival from work and I was able to re-pot it without any problem. Chuckling to myself, I fashioned a cover out of hardware cloth (half-inch wire mesh) and secured it to the pot. So much for that problem! There would be no further damage to THAT plant. The next day I discovered the rose tree...actually the stalk minus the roots and upper foliage with the blooming roses...but luckily Hilde was unharmed. Well, okay, maybe she really wasn't perfect after all.

Chapter 5

Adolescence

Work continued on Hilde's leash training and most weekends I took her out to the power plant to take advantage of the many different sights, sounds and smells. She was fascinated by the seagulls and would follow their movements for long periods of time. I never considered that the sight of the birds might have been stirring and reinforcing some of her basic hunting instincts, especially since these were SEAGULLS. The myriad sounds and movement of equipment and personnel taught her acceptance of things far beyond the relative safety of her own backyard. Her self-confidence grew with each new wonderful discovery. At times she seemed to just stand and absorb things happening around her. It was obvious that she relished those trips.

The power plant provided another great opportunity: there is one walkway that was perfect for setting the correct lateral distance for Hilde as she walked on a leash. Soon she was walking perfectly both on and off leash. By arriving just before the security shift change, she could meet personnel from both shifts. Two ladies, Sue and Morgan, were her favorites. They would kneel then just say her name and she would rush to them. "Watch out, she won't...never mind. Sorry. Here, let me help you up."

Morgan once stopped her vehicle in the middle of the street having just spotted Hilde and me taking a walk. She called Hilde's name and Hilde yanked the leash out of my hand then rushed to Morgan. Morgan had checked for traffic prior to stopping (thankfully) and I learned yet another lesson about the power of certain voices.

Sometimes I would take Hilde inside the Support

Building at the plant and let her walk on and off leash. She detected every single morsel of food that had been placed in a trashcan or other location. She also managed to sniff all sorts of known and unknown items with complete confidence. She was able to quickly locate those areas that I frequented on a regular basis and that must have been a comforting influence in this new environment.

The elevators were another surprise...no fear or hesitation whatsoever. She was a little confused the first time she stepped out of the elevator on the second floor...my scent was not apparent and she moved perhaps ten feet before stopping and looking at me. When I moved in the direction of my office area (which was actually one floor below), she raced away with great confidence, slowed and then stopped. She looked at me and I motioned for her to continue. Instead, she walked to me and we returned to the elevator. Upon exiting on the first floor, she hesitated and then raced to my office area. I arrived to find a very happy Hilde now fully at ease again. The elevator was clearly magic; the stairs were no concern except that she could not open the doors.

On one occasion, I introduced her to the security Shift Commander by name and repeated it several times. Hilde and I then adjourned to another part of the building while the Shift Commander continued with some of his paperwork. When we were at the furthermost part of the building, I told Hilde to "Go find Eric." Hilde raced away and I followed at a much slower pace. Soon I heard Eric's muffled voice and as I approached I could hear him talking to her! She excelled at this game much to the delight of anyone who ever played it. She could usually associate the name with the scent for two days before she forgot the name; she could remember the scent much longer.

On another occasion, I was experiencing some computer problems at home and asked a co-worker for help. Gene and Hilde were introduced to each other and then each went about his/her own business. After a few minutes, I told Hilde to go see Gene and she rushed to him. I did this several times and each time he would pause to visit with her. He stayed for dinner and played with her until time to leave. Hilde followed him to the door and watched his departure. Several hours later I asked her to find Gene and she went to the window and looked for him. This went on for two days, but by the third day she seemed to have forgotten his name. Their next encounter was more than one year later and she remembered his voice and rushed to him.

I had read a little about tracking dogs and how some dogs excelled while others never picked up the concept. Out came the smoked jerky, which I tied to a string. I dragged it through the front yard, across the driveway and over into the side yard making several turns. I then removed the string and left the jerky on a leaf. I brought Hilde to the starting point and she followed the trail to the piece of jerky without losing the scent trail even once. I was convinced that tracking would be part of her future and we practiced on a regular basis. We did mental games also.

Hilde had a series of toys that she knew by name. The outside toys were often thrown into her wading pool where she would retrieve them by sticking her head under water, picking them up and bringing them to us. Okay, let me explain the wading pool: it was there for her to cool off if necessary while letting her become comfortable in a water environment. We were not yet ready to take her to the nearby pond for some serious swimming. Her favorite water toy was a yellow plastic duck with a squeaker. This toy endured her daily assaults with no sign of wear and tear. Since it floated, she had to work harder to retrieve it. So we would send her after the boat, bone, tug, ring, ball and ducky. After a few days she began using her paws to drag the specified toy to the edge of the pool, pull it up the side and lift it out of the water so that she could grasp it in her mouth. It was obvious that she learned things quickly. There were two ways to end the game: walk away or offer her part of a juice bar and she always preferred the juice bar option.

Her inside toys were usually made of canvas plus she had some nylon chewing toys which were supposedly good for her teeth...and of course she hated those. The canvas toys were her favorites until she discovered tennis balls. She always remembered where her toys were and it was fun to tell her to go find "baby" or "kitty." We always used such snappy names! Hilde would return with the correct toy and await whatever game was to be played. Inside toys were exactly that and she would not take them outside. Outside toys were a different matter and she always tried (and still tries) to sneak them inside. There is probably some reason but we have not been able to figure it out.

We purchased a doghouse with a soft, clear plastic door which she removed the first day. Still not content with her house, she made the opening a little wider by removing excess material from both lower sections of the door opening. Her final touch was to lower the very bottom portion of the entrance, perhaps so that she wouldn't be forced to lift her paws quite so high on entry and departure. Once these modifications had been completed she was content with her custom doghouse. Notice the absence of the phrase "perfect puppy."

We continued our ritual of constant photographs and were surprised to notice that Hilde was very much aware of the camera. If she detected the presence of the camera, she would immediately turn toward it and remain motionless until the flash fired. She became somewhat confused if there was no flash and would simply wait until the photographer moved. After that she continued with her own agenda. One other similar change concerned her actions that generated laughter...if you laughed, she would either repeat or intensify whatever action had brought on the laughter. She thoroughly enjoyed the spotlight.

Hilde continued to grow and we waited for the magic day when she would be six months old. This was significant because she would then be able to compete in AKC dog shows. Part of the co-ownership deal with the breeder was that she would show Hilde until she obtained champion status. We were anxious to reach this major milestone.

When Hilde finally reached the ripe old age of six months, we commenced our telephone vigil. Sue never called so we called her and told her how much we would like for her to look at Hilde hoping for some serious ring training. We worked out a time and date and took Hilde to see Sue. Somehow Sue did not share in our enthusiasm and did not seem particularly impressed with Hilde. She commented on everything except showing her. All training books stress the importance of teaching your puppy to come, sit and stay. We demonstrated how Hilde would sit and were promptly informed that you NEVER TEACH A SHOW DOG TO SIT. Well, silly us! It was no use to explain that Hilde would sit on a verbal or hand signal, but you could not force her to sit. We also mentioned her tracking prowess and were informed that you NEVER TEACH A SHOW DOG TO TRACK. This visit was going nowhere fast. Sue did explain that a dog that is taught to sit might do so in the ring if the head is lifted with the leash or if downward pressure is applied to the hips. She further explained that some dogs do not carry their heads high enough in the ring and tracking detracts from that plus there is already too much interesting stuff on the ground or floor to distract the dog anyway. Sue stated that she would like to look at Hilde again later. We were crushed. No praise, no comments or indications that we had done anything right. Other than that, it was a good visit. (Just trying to stay positive.)

We saw a need to provide Hilde with a method of getting exercise and reducing her boredom when she was home alone. One new toy had appeared by accident: we had left an empty one-gallon plastic water jug out in the yard. Hilde had picked it up by the handle and began charging around the yard with her vision partially blocked by the jug. It was truly a funny sight. She would fall and release her grip on the handle. This was followed by an immediate pounce on the jug which usually collapsed under her weight. She would then grab the handle and repeat the process. Unfortunately, Hilde began to chew the jugs and we chose to remove them from her arsenal of toys.

We needed something a little safer. Our solution was to string a cable between two trees outside opposite sides of the fenced yard. A pulley with a knotted rope toy was attached and was free to roll along the cable. A spring on each end of the cable provided enough tension to keep the cable up and also provided some "give." Stops located about ten feet from each end of the cable prevented Hilde from running into the fence. It did not take more than two or three exposures to this arrangement before she found a fun way to amuse herself.

If we were home, we would simply grab the knotted rope and sling it as far as possible; Hilde would race to the rope and grab it. From there she did various things. Sometimes she simply brought it back to us for a repeat. Other times she would tug perpendicular to the cable pulling against the springs and then release the rope which would fly in the opposite direction. She would immediately go after it and repeat the process over and over. At other times I would grab the cable and cause the knotted rope to jump or twirl while Hilde attempted to grab it. Some of her acrobatics were unbelievable and she could play this game until I was forced to quit due to exhaustion. Her strength and agility grew steadily and her muscle tone was incredible.

Hilde developed one habit that caught us off guard. She loved to chew the small pieces of waste concrete that were left behind from the fence construction. We picked up every piece that we could find and she switched to small rocks from a sandy portion of the yard. The vet was not worried so we slowed our rock removal activities and she stopped. Our joy was quickly shattered...she began digging! No one ever witnessed her digging a hole, but the holes appeared nevertheless. I usually took Hilde over to the freshly dug hole and asked, "Who did this?" She would lower her head and give her best expression of remorse and then DO IT AGAIN THE NEXT DAY! We finally discovered a trend: there was always a rock roughly the size of a tennis ball in the hole and it was usually about eight or ten inches below ground level. How she knew that there was a rock in that exact location remains a mystery. Did these rocks make sounds with temperature changes? Did they have some irresistible odor? Was it simply coincidence?

There was one exception to the buried rock trend: she once discovered a metal, cylindrical object at a depth of approximately one-foot. I was unable to immediately check it due to other priorities and the idea of previous owners' buried items became a lively topic. Cash? Old coins? What could it be? It turned out to be an old engine oil filter. Hilde the Treasure Finder had been granted a reprieve from the digging warnings, but they immediately resumed.

Our plan was to stop the digging; we HAD to stop the digging. We tried holding her nose in the hole and scolding her...that was useless. Someone recommended filling the hole with water and holding her head in the hole...I could not do that. Finally the solution appeared by accident.

Every dog owner knows what collects in the yard when you own a dog. For those of you who don't know, does the phrase "Watch your step" provide a vivid image? Periodically this ownership by-product must be picked up for disposal. We suddenly realized that we had a source of burial locations provided by Hilde herself! It worked, although initially she just relocated to another spot for digging activities. She gave up after a couple of weeks. Actually, she still manages an occasional relapse, but nothing compared to her earlier performances.

Her next major surprise concerned notifying us when she needed to go out or come in. Initially, she would simply go to the back door and sit on the mat and quietly wait. If we failed to notice, she would find one of us and then walk back to her waiting spot. We did not always pick up on this subtle hint and she learned to strike the latch with her nose. She was not able to unlatch the door, but at least we could hear her signal. She would repeat it as necessary until we finally opened the door. When it was time to come back in she just stood on the back steps and scratched on the door. It was a good system and was relatively quiet; she never barked for entrance or exit.

We took Hilde many places either in my pickup truck or in our Saturn coupe. For her safety, we purchased a harness, which hooked to the seatbelt system. She was able to crawl out of it in seconds no matter how tightly she was strapped in. I soon built a padded platform for the back seat of the Saturn. It was level and much more comfortable for her. Unfortunately, she preferred the front seat or if Bobbie and I were both in the car, she wanted to sprawl over the center console. A small barrier solved that problem. She never harmed any part of the car and became a great traveling companion. Teaching her to "go" on command had been a great idea and was especially beneficial if we took her on a long trip. Gee, if it had only worked with daughters Debbie and Donna!

Somewhere along this point in her life we noticed that in the mornings while Bobbie and I were getting ready to go to work that Hilde preferred to lie on her back on the bed and watch us. It apparently did not bother her to look at us while she was upside down. As long as we gave her some attention she was fine. On one occasion Bobbie just stared at her without saying anything. Hilde suddenly commenced crying in a long, melodious manner. "Honey, Hilde is singing." From that point on, you only needed to tell Hilde to "sing" and she would! Of course, if you joined in, she would make it a contest...and the more the merrier! She would try to duplicate your pitch changes and it was only a matter of time until you were laughing so hard that you couldn't continue. Looking back, I'm sure that at least one neighbor must have wondered what was going on and was probably glad when cold weather arrived and the bedroom windows were closed. Hilde only "sang" while lying on her back and her only other vocalization performed on command was "speak," which was not especially remarkable except that she would only do that if she was sitting.

Bobbie flew down to Florida for a visit with her folks and I decided to take Hilde with me when I picked her up at the airport. I knew the flight number and expected arrival time and tried to plan my arrival so that she could grab her luggage and meet me curbside. Hilde and I made two circuits of the arrival area without spotting Bobbie. At that point I decided to ask one of the State Troopers who monitor the pick-up area if I could leave the car just long enough to run inside and check the arrival time to see if the flight had been delayed. It was well past the heavy arrival time period and I thought that it was a reasonable request. As I pulled to a stop, the State Trooper walked over and I lowered my window. Immediately Hilde commenced her most ferocious barking. This made communication extremely difficult and I attempted to calm Hilde and stop her barking. The State Trooper was clearly annoyed by this vicious animal and was anything but relaxed. When she finally quieted, I made my request. The answer was a non-negotiable "No!"

By this time the Trooper had knelt beside the car and Hilde no longer considered him to be a threat. Soon she was sniffing and then licking his hand. I pleaded my case a second time hoping that he would relent. He didn't. I reminded him that there was no other traffic and he told me to move on or Hilde and I would both be arrested. I drove away and looked back in my mirror: he was shaking his head and grinning from ear to ear. And so I drove around again thinking that he might have changed his mind. I asked if he had a change of heart and he smiled and said, "Yes, I'll arrest you and KEEP the dog." We both laughed and he asked Hilde's name and then told her that she was a good dog, but should never bark at law enforcement personnel. That exchange made it more palatable when I parked in the general parking area.

Chapter 6

Still Growing

As summer changed to fall we began to address the difficulties associated with the oncoming winter. Snow and extreme cold could be a real problem for Hilde. Time spent inside the house should not be a concern, but outdoor activities might be dangerous. Hilde's short coat would offer little protection from severe cold and even though her doghouse was insulated, it might not provide sufficient protection. At nights she would be in the house, but the days were our concern since we would be at work. Typical winters in our area never produced bitter cold for more than a few days at a time. Bobbie and I agreed that Hilde would remain in the house if there was ANY question about cold weather.

Some time in late October I noticed some wooden shingles missing from the side of the house. I noticed that they were only missing from a height less than four feet above ground level. I retrieved several broken shingles and noticed the teeth marks. Moments later Hilde appeared with part of one of the shingles in her mouth. I grabbed the shingle and tried the "No, no...bad dog" routine. Hilde showed instant remorse by dropping her head and looking sheepish. I thought I had solved that problem rather nicely and decided to repair the damage on the following weekend. The next day Hilde greeted me with a shingle in her mouth even though I was certain that I had picked up each one the day before. Surprise! It became clear that my weekend repair task was now much larger. I tried various things to break her of this habit but was unable to stop the damage. I replaced the missing and damaged shingles and installed a low powered electric fence designed specifically for

40

pets. I routed it along the two sides of the house where she had access and the problem was solved. I never saw her touch the wire but she obviously must have touched it at some point and we soon unplugged the unit leaving the wires in place. No more shingle damage!

One of Hilde's delights was to jump up on the picnic table. Perhaps this was to make her taller so that she could more easily look us in the eye. At first she utilized the benches, but as she grew she was able to leap directly to the tabletop. This also made her more visible from inside. I would sometimes catch Bobbie staring at Hilde through the kitchen window with a smile on her face. The two maintained eye contact as if they were sharing some special secret or dream. It was a wonderful sight. I was never included in this special rite with either Bobbie or Hilde. Eventually I gave up and quit sitting on the picnic table.

November arrived bringing cooler weather. Raking leaves was both fun and aggravating if Hilde happened to be nearby. She loved to destroy the piles of leaves! The first few times were hilarious but soon became tedious. Finally, she was banned from the leaf raking area until all leaves were bagged. (Mental note: REMOVE the plastic bags BEFORE allowing Hilde back out into the yard!) November also brought our first frost and a learning experience for Hilde.

I went outside with Hilde early one morning and noticed the frost on everything. She made her morning rounds and then raced back to me only to decide at the last instant to leap upon the picnic table as she had done so many times before. When she hit the frost covered tabletop she did not slow down at all! The strangest expression was on her face as she continued along the table. I almost laughed. Upon reaching the end she gently dropped to the ground and slowly returned to the picnic table. She eased herself onto one of the benches and checked the surface of the table. She sniffed it and stared at it for several seconds and then looked at me as if to ask, "What happened?" We did not see her jump on the picnic table for several days after that.

The first time her water dish froze was clearly confusing to her. She immediately ran to her wading pool and encountered the same problem with the water. Without hesitation she leaped into the wading pool and broke through the ice. She destroyed the remainder of the ice projecting from the sides by biting it off. Having accomplished that she returned to the back door and indicated that she was ready to come in. As the day warmed, she checked the wading pool and apparently associated the disappearance of the ice with her actions to break it up. The same thing occurred several times with identical results. Eventually we experienced a hard freeze and no matter how hard she tried, she could not break through the ice. We were certain that we would not see her ice breaking routine again, but she always held on to her belief that she COULD break through the ice. Watching her tap dance on the frozen surface was great fun. The brand new, heated water dish worked fine...except Hilde wouldn't drink the water!

The first snowfall was a source of absolute joy for Hilde. Initially she tried to eat every snowflake within reach. Then she went after only the largest flakes, leaping as high as possible. As the snowfall became heavier, she ran through the falling snow with reckless abandon as if possessed. She refused to come inside until she was completely exhausted. After a lengthy nap she was once again ready to go out. By then the snow was deep enough that she was clearly confused...only the fence and the picnic table were clearly discernible. The snow must have felt different and she shook each paw several times perhaps in an attempt to restore some semblance of normalcy. After a few minutes she gave up and began a slow trot through the yard. Her confidence rapidly grew and she made several fast circuits around the yard and stopped. She then lowered her head and ran across the yard with her mouth open, gathering snow in her mouth. She stopped, ate it and resumed her forward motion only this time her mouth was closed. To this day, if she has been out in the snow, she will have a small bit of snow on her nose.

Hilde always loved to play in the snow either alone or with one of us. Taking her for walks on a leash became more difficult in bad weather for several reasons. Although she received considerable exercise in the back yard, she still had tremendous energy and the leash became a mere inconvenience as she pulled her way along! It took several minutes before she would settle down and walk properly on the leash. This was especially hazardous to the person on the other end of the leash due to the slippery conditions. Outside the confines of the yard there was no possibility of letting her run loose; she had recently discovered that if she refused to return when called, she could get by with it. So it was now necessary to wear her down and then perhaps you could at least jog with her. She checked every scent trail she encountered and on snow or ice she had the advantage...her version of four wheel drive. I always considered these outings as exercise for the two of us; she considered them as explorations and she was always far more enthusiastic than I.

We never knowingly taught Hilde any aggressive behavior. Sure we played rough with her, but even games like tug of war were always won by the two-legged members of her pack. She never exhibited any aggressive or protective tendencies whatsoever. That changed one day while Bobbie and I were standing in the living room discussing some minor thing. Suddenly Bobbie playfully struck me on the shoulder with her fist. She withdrew her fist and attempted to tap me again. She never touched me. From out of nowhere a gray streak leaped into the air grabbing her wrist! Bobbie was spun around with her arm extended and locked in Hilde's mouth! Hilde released Bobbie's wrist immediately and had left no marks. Why had she attacked? We both realized that Hilde had considered the tap on my shoulder to be an attack on me. Had she protected me?

We waited several minutes and repeated the

performance only this time I was the one tapping Bobbie on the shoulder. Hilde grabbed my wrist on the second attempt to "strike" Bobbie and the momentum of her leap spun me around and forced me to move along with her. She held my wrist in her mouth and looked at me with remorse, but did not release me until I said her name. Although I had been unable to remove my wrist from her grip, she had not broken the skin. Hilde only feared what my actions would be since I was her "pack leader" and she had attacked me. I praised her and whether that was right or wrong has not been an issue at our house. Her instincts had been to stop the attack. I do not believe that Hilde thought she was ATTACKING ME but, rather, that she was actually PROTECTING BOBBIE. That raised a question regarding her actions should she encountered one of us in an injured status. Would she recognize an injured person?

We have a basement with inside access and Hilde would not go down those steps. I even carried her down once and though she easily climbed out, she simply refused to go down the steps. From the basement you can trace the footsteps of anyone moving through the house. I was down in the basement for some long forgotten reason and had left the door open. Periodically, Hilde would wander by and peer down at me. Once, after she left, I decided to check her reaction to a staged "accident." I carefully set up some cans and other objects which would made some noise. I could tell that Bobbie was in the kitchen at the sink and Hilde was either in the living room or kitchen. I knocked the cans over and quickly assumed a facedown position on the cellar floor with my head resting on the first cellar step. I heard Hilde coming and softly groaned. She uttered a feeble "yip" and raced into the kitchen. I heard Bobbie say something to Hilde but could not understand it. Seconds later Hilde returned and there was that "yip" again. More groans and Hilde raced away and seconds later I heard Bobbie heading my way. I shouted that it was all fake and that I was okay and went back to groaning. Hilde came down the stairs and tried her best to get me to move...that was a shock. After a miraculous "recovery," I was able to slowly arise and climb those steps and praise that wonderful dog that had just "saved my life." Bobbie and I were once again pleasantly surprised.

Two days later we repeated the performance for Michael with similar results and he was equally impressed. Hilde was now a cellar stairs climbing machine and used any opportunity to run up and down the stairs. Perhaps a little jealous, Bobbie wondered aloud if Hilde would summon help if SHE were injured in the cellar. Once again we set up the cans and other props and Bobbie remained in the cellar while Hilde and I returned to the living room. After several minutes there was a loud crash and Hilde bolted to the cellar door. I heard her footsteps on the stairs followed by a brief silence. Suddenly she came charging up the stairs and I grinned in anticipation of her arrival and her possible methods of indicating that I should follow her to the cellar! What a wonderful dog! Hilde continued into the living room and then into the kitchen and clicked the door latch...She needed to go out!! Okay, maybe she was just nervous. I let her out, she emptied her bladder and returned. I opened the door and she went back to the living room and curled up on the loveseat! Simultaneously, Bobbie asked what was happening. Hilde and I went to the cellar door and I explained what had happened. I thought it was hilarious; Bobbie was crushed. We never did that drill again. (But it's still funny.)

Hilde continued along her path of endearment. As the weather warmed and the days grew longer, I seized the opportunity to finish the final repairs to the shingles that she had previously destroyed. Once that was completed I decided to apply a coat of linseed oil to the shingles as a possible deterrent. Hilde would not leave the linseed oil container alone and it became necessary to put her on a long leash. Once I had her situated so that she could not create more havoc, I resumed transferring the linseed oil to my working container. In less than a minute Hilde was at my side, bumping against the container! Attached to her collar was an eighteen-inch section of her woven leash. I repaired the leash and returned her to her previous location; by the time I reached the linseed oil container she had already sliced through the leash and was on her way over to assist me! The brand new, lightweight chain worked fine! It was never used again. Oh, and Hilde did not mind the flavor of linseed oil. And thus the wires from the electric pet fence remained in place even though we had thrown the transformer away.

Chapter 7

Hilde Turns One

Bailey was a yellow Labrador Retriever who lived next door. Hilde always played with her through the fence and they got along exceptionally well. They would bark at each other in play but never in a confrontational role. Bailey's owners would often allow their other neighbors' dog to come over to play with Bailey and both dogs seemed to thoroughly enjoy themselves. It was logical to think that Bailey would play well with Hilde.

One day while Bernie, our neighbor, was walking Bailey, I asked if he would bring her over so the two dogs could play in our yard. He agreed and there was no problem until the gate closed. In a split second Bailey was on her back with Hilde at her throat! Bailey was not injured but that ended any future hope of the two dogs playing in our yard. Bernie and I discussed the territorial aspects and I asked if I could bring Hilde over to his yard thinking that Hilde would behave there. Bernie declined having just witnessed The World's Most Vicious Weimaraner in action and we were never able to see if that would have worked out. There would be a future surprise, but I'll cover that later.

The Playmate For Hilde movement ended almost as quickly as it had begun...or did it? Perhaps she did need a companion and there was certainly room for another dog. Bobbie and I began justifying a puppy for Hilde. The reasons were endless and we both conveniently left out the obvious: WE WANTED ANOTHER WEIMIE. The stage was set and it was only a matter of time until we contacted Sue at Camelot Kennels.

Once we made the decision to obtain our second dog we went through much of the same soul-searching as with

Hilde. By this time we knew that Hilde was an "alpha" type and that we could probably not have a second female. Thus we were in the market for a male. Breeding our own male and female was not our intention so bloodlines were not an issue. We just wanted a male with good demeanor. Of course it wouldn't hurt if he were an exceptionally nice specimen.

We never discussed the possibility of checking with another breeder; Camelot Kennels had served us well. Now the question was when did we want to bring home a puppy. Sometime around mid-June would be perfect and since puppies usually went to their new homes at eight weeks of age, the puppy should be born in mid-April. We definitely did not want a puppy born in the fall due to the proximity of winter. What if we had to go the co-ownership route? Did we want the restrictions and limitations? We had experienced no real impact from Hilde's co-ownership and were ready to accept it if out-right full ownership was not possible. We contacted Sue and she stated that she had a litter due in late April and that those puppies should be available. She recommended a male due to the probable conflict with another female and we congratulated ourselves on our foresight. Now it was hurry up and wait. Hey, that sounded familiar!

Hilde had reached her adult height and was just filling out her width. Her weight was becoming stable and now it was time to concentrate on keeping it right at optimum. She always had room for food and it was critical to monitor her weight and make adjustments for her physical exertion levels. Michael had begun using a hockey stick to launch tennis balls for her to catch or retrieve. Hilde would even forego her evening meal to chase those tennis balls. That was her favorite activity and Michael would always tire before she did. Her agility continued to impress us. She made a great goalie.

Hilde waited for Michael to arrive home from work each day and, like most dogs, was able to estimate his arrival time very accurately. On those days that Michael worked late or had other priorities, Hilde would wait patiently and slowly become more restless as the anticipated arrival time arrived and then passed. She would become distraught and either Bobbie or I would go out and hit or throw the ball. The purpose of the hockey stick is quickly understood by anyone who has picked up and thrown a tennis ball more than five or six times if bare ground exists! Hilde began greeting Michael at the door with a tennis ball in her mouth. If you were in the cellar and Michael was late, you would hear the "thump, thump, thump, etc." of a tennis ball coming down the stairs as a reminder that it was THAT time. In Hilde's view, tennis balls and someone to launch them provided her with the best that life had to offer.

At approximately the same point in her life, our fearless (I really DO mean fearless) Hilde encountered something that she just could not comprehend. Thunderstorms are not especially common in our area and we had been particularly lucky to have not encountered one since Hilde's arrival. The first one was distant and caused no real concern on her part. The next one was very close and while the flash of lightning was not a problem, the thunder was. Hilde was terrified and shaking violently; she could not be distracted or consoled. She had always rejected Michael's room as a place to stay or visit. Suddenly this was where she wanted to go! Hilde was not seen (voluntarily) until the thunder had subsided for some time. She emerged from Michael's room very cautiously and ready to return if necessary. This was the first time I had seen her express any type of fear. Typically, if she could SEE something new or strange...it was somehow acceptable and not a cause for alarm. I believe that if she had been able to understand the relationship between lightning and thunder that she could have accepted the thunder. I know that dogs have some reasoning powers, but I do not believe them to be extensive.

There was another demon that plagued Hilde and does so even today. Usually we know when to expect this one and can take steps to alleviate the situation. A nuclear power plant is required to have a notification system to inform local inhabitants of any imminent danger from the plant. This Public Address system uses powerful speaker systems to broadcast warning sirens and verbal directions. The actual employment of this system is exceedingly rare, but testing is done on a regular basis. On one occasion I had taken the day off and was home when a partial test of the system (or perhaps just the unit located less than half a block from our house) was conducted. I was outside and Hilde was nearby when a very loud voice stated, "This is a test." The rotating speaker array was pointed straight at us and believe me, it was loud!

In the shortest measure of time known to man, Hilde traveled perhaps twenty feet to my side. I was extremely thankful that she had finally learned to stop. She then timidly peeked around my legs to find the source of the voice. Of course she was not able to see anyone and it would have been a VERY LARGE someone to have a voice that loud. She slowly began to relax. Seconds later there was a slight crackle followed by, "Test, test, test." Hilde hesitated for a split second preferring to remain at my side, but the 'fight or flight' decision was quickly rendered because THERE WAS NO ONE TO FIGHT! The scratches in the back door remain even to this day. I could not drag her out of Michael's room. She had absolutely no problem with police cars, ambulances and fire trucks because she had SEEN them. Perhaps to Hilde the thunder and the speaker voice were the canine equivalents of the Voice of God and it was clearly evident that she was a God-fearing dog!

* *

Hilde was approaching her first birthday which was no big deal until Bobbie jokingly asked Michael if he would be attending Hilde's birthday party. Thinking that she was serious, Michael cringed at the thought of such a spectacle and that was all it took! Bobbie and I decided to throw her a real birthday party. Bobbie ordered a cake and I picked up the necessary items to decorate the house and especially the dining room...something that is not normally done at our house. We bought Hilde some gifts and carefully wrapped them so that she could open them by herself; we included a small treat to provide extra motivation. All of these preparations were kept from Michael until the very end. The snickering was really hard to contain! We knew that his girlfriend would be there and would be happy to join us for the celebration.

The big day arrived and that evening after dinner we quickly decorated the house, set up the gifts, put the camcorder on the tripod and readied the other camera. The dining room table held the gifts and the guest of honor sat on the bench next to Bobbie; both were wearing party hats...the kind with the rubber band used as a chinstrap. That was guaranteed to drive Michael up the walls! The cake was in the shape of a bone and had "Happy Birthday Hilde" on it. A single candle in the shape of the numeral "one" adorned the cake. I put on my own party hat, put the camcorder on "record" and we invited Michael and Shannon to share in this joyous occasion. Michael was appalled and I suppose that our laughter didn't help!

Bobbie lit the candle and invited everyone to sing "Happy Birthday." There was only one individual who chose not to sing along, but I would not be so rude as to mention him by name. Hilde looked on in awe as the candle burned and the singing continued. Actually, Bobbie had to physically restrain her since she could smell the treats hidden in the nearby gifts. Of course Bobbie (and not Hilde) blew out the candle and it was suddenly time to open the gifts. The camcorder was running constantly and I took this opportunity to pick up my regular camera to grab at least one snapshot of this strange celebration. Hilde opened one gift which contained a canvas kitty. She grabbed the kitty instead of the treat and I chose that instant to raise my camera and call her name. She turned, saw the camera and tilted her head up with the kitty's legs and tail dangling from her mouth and held that pose. As soon as the flash fired, she dropped the kitty and grabbed the treat. Everyone burst out laughing and, luckily, the whole episode was captured on tape.

Hilde continued opening her gifts and posed for each photo. We attempted to coax Michael and Shannon to pose with Bobbie and Hilde while I took a group photo. Reluctantly, Michael finally agreed and in a small act of defiance, pushed Bobbie's hat sideways toward Hilde. Hilde instantly turned and pushed the hat back to its original position with her nose! More laughter. I couldn't believe my eyes! That was also captured on tape.

Bobbie cut the cake and offered a small piece to the guest of honor. Although the camcorder was operating perfectly, looking through the viewfinder I did not see Hilde eat that piece of cake. There was a piece of cake on a plate, a blur and suddenly the piece of cake was gone. We had to call for a retake and a re-cake! Hilde was starting to like this experience! After the second piece of cake, we released Hilde who would not allow us to remove her hat...she was having too much fun and her hat must somehow be causing it. We took a few photos of our "party animal" and cleaned up the mess. After that experience, Hilde would allow virtually anything to be placed on her head! Michael refused to view the tape with us.

Happy birthday, Hilde. The wait for the puppy continued.

Chapter 8

Blade

It was June before we knew for certain that the litter with our puppy was soon to be available. There were four males and one female...at least this time the numbers were in our favor. We had reached agreement on a name: Blade. There was no special meaning attached...it just sounded good. Of course we would also need an AKC name and Sue required "Camelot" to be part of that name. So we decided that Camelot's Excalibur would be Blade's AKC name. It was simple, elegant and tied both names together. We visited the kennel and saw the puppies at the age of three weeks but were unable to tell much except that they were healthy. We returned four weeks later at Sue's urging to look at them and possibly make our selection. Sue would not be there...she had a dog show that weekend. Oh, and co-ownership was a requirement.

Eric, her son, brought all five puppies out into the grassy area near the parking lot and placed them in a small portable pen. Bobbie entered the pen and sat in the middle. We watched as the puppies approached her. Four came to her almost immediately while one with wrinkled skin on his head stayed back but eventually overcame his shyness. Bobbie spent thirty minutes in that pen even lying on her back while the now-confident puppies crawled all over her. She was laughing and thoroughly enjoying this very special time. I recorded the whole episode with a camcorder, trying to catch each puppy at various angles for comparison. All five were virtually identical in size and only two stood out: the only female for obvious reasons and the male with the wrinkled skin on his head. Otherwise, the puppies were essentially identical. There was no real way that we could pick out the best puppy, but then we couldn't lose...any of the males would be perfect.

Sue called that Sunday night and asked what we thought of the puppies. We mentioned that we were unable to pick one and she stated that they were all so close that even she had difficulty trying to pick the best puppy. We were not concerned since all four males were so close in all respects and only one seemed just a little bit shy compared to the others; he was the one with the wrinkles on his head. We knew that we would be happy with any of the four males. Sue called a few days later and said we could pick up our puppy. Her mentor, Judy Colan, had stopped in and they had the opportunity to look at all five puppies at the age when their proportions approximate that of their adult look. As a result of this final scrutiny, Sue had picked our puppy.

We arrived at the kennel that Saturday and Eric informed us of the color of the collar of our puppy. With that we rushed out to the puppy "house" and located Blade...he had wrinkles on his head! He was lying at the door of the house looking out. We slowly and carefully made our way into the building and picked up Blade who seemed not the least bit distraught. We held and petted him for a few minutes then went up to the office to complete the required paperwork. And then, armed with paperwork, food and medications, we departed with Blade and drove home. Not a whimper, but then Bobbie would not let him go; she held him for the entire trip. We arrived home to a very anxious Michael and a very curious Hilde. Blade was exactly eight weeks old.

We had been assured by Sue that there would not be any problems with Hilde during her introduction to Blade. Even so, we were extremely cautious and reluctant to leave them alone together. Their first meeting was in the house with Blade being held by Bobbie. Hilde was allowed to approach and was trembling with excitement. She would not stop sniffing and her tail was wagging so there was no reason to suspect any problems. It was clear that Hilde was very happy to have another dog in her pack.

After the introductions, we adjourned to the back yard and placed Blade on the ground. Hilde flattened him almost immediately and he uttered a pathetic little cry. Three voices simultaneously shouted, "Hilde, no!" Blade got up and Hilde was all over him, sniffing and wagging her tail and then easing off. A bewildered Blade then began an attempted exploration of the yard followed closely by Hilde. Periodically, Hilde would block his progress and you could see the fear reflected in his demeanor. This continued for several minutes as we watched in nervous agony. We knew that this was something to simply endure and that soon this ordeal would be over and the two would (hopefully) get along well.

Hilde alternated between soft growls and joyous whining as Blade either moved toward her or waddled away. Within thirty minutes Hilde was showing curiosity only and was willing to let Blade explore in peace. She had made her point about being in charge. Soon Hilde was enticing Blade to play by carrying a toy past him. On those few occasions where he grabbed the toy, she yanked it from his mouth apparently unaware that he was not as strong or as fast as she. It was clear that she wanted to play, but was unable to convince him.

Blade slept well that night. We had played with him and kept him awake as much as possible. Finally it was time to put him to bed and see what would happen. He was in his own small crate near Hilde. He was perfectly quiet and went to sleep almost immediately. We did get up once to let him outside and all went well. Perhaps we would be as fortunate in housebreaking Blade as we were with Hilde. This was not to be the case...Blade took two weeks. His problem was simply not letting us know. We always took him out after naps or after eating or drinking, but he just surprised us at times. Then out of the clear blue he caught on and never had another accident.

The second day started off with a curious Hilde checking Blade. Good grief, Hilde, he's the same puppy from yesterday! After a few minutes she relaxed and went about her own routine while we watched. She still spent a lot of time sniffing, but there were no more altercations and we were confident that we could go to work the next day with no worries. Feeding was not a problem as long as we kept Hilde away. It would be a long time before we could feed both dogs simultaneously without Hilde being restrained either verbally or physically.

We called Sue to verify that Camelot's Excalibur was an acceptable name for AKC purposes and were informed that there had been a previous dog by that name. Time to start over. We could not come up with anything. Sue called back later...Judy Colan had suggested Camelot's Cutting Edge. That was it! We had our name! We completed the paperwork and mailed it to the AKC. Blade was almost named KENO (after a nice winning payoff), but common sense and reality intervened and saved the day.

* *

Imprinting is a process where a puppy undergoes some experience at an early age and it becomes a part of him forever. Discipline by the mother is certainly one of those. Many breeders of the pointing and retrieving breeds expose their puppies to the scent of a gamebird at an early age so that the hunting instinct develops just in case the new owner is looking for that trait. So it was with both Hilde and Blade. Hilde, however, was not exposed to swimming. I could only describe her swimming style as "beating the water into submission." It was not a pretty sight; actually, it was down right embarrassing. Hilde just would not or could not swim with that smooth cadence that I had always seen in other dogs. Therefore it was necessary to see if water imprinting would work with Blade. We had purchased a child's swimming pool which was deep enough and Blade's second day at home was the target date. We made certain that the water was warm so that the experience would not be too traumatic and I carefully supported his body. He immediately commenced paddling and after several trials we stopped for the day. It was a good experience and he especially enjoyed the toweling dry and the extra attention that came with it.

One week later we went to a nearby pond with both dogs and let Blade play at the edge of the water for a considerable amount of time. I worked with Hilde trying to smooth out her style. Either she didn't take her instruction well or her instructor was just plain incompetent...she simply churned the water to froth.

At some point in time it was Blade's turn. I carried him out into deeper water and eased him lower and lower until he automatically began paddling. I gradually released him completely and he swam approximately five feet until his feet touched bottom and he walked to shore and began exploring. Several minutes later I repeated the process and he swam about ten feet. He was very smooth with just his head exposed and no signs of being distraught. That was enough for the day; I did not want him to become excessively tired or have a bad experience. Once again he loved being dried by a towel. On subsequent visits to the pond he demonstrated the capability of retrieving submerged rocks, yet I never saw him retrieve a submerged toy from the wading pool.

Unlike Hilde, Blade did not run to you when called; he walked with great purpose. He was more laid back and saw no urgency in going or coming. Leash training was easy and he was soon walking perfectly on or off leash. I once again utilized the power plant for much of his new experiences and noticed that unlike Hilde, Blade was not loaded with confidence. We had already noticed that he was somewhat more shy than his siblings and assumed that he would change in his new environment. In retrospect, Hilde must have been far rougher on him than his siblings. We changed our strategy and began to expose him to new experiences, but tried to spot the disasters before they occurred. We wanted him to have these new experiences without traumatizing him in the process. Usually we succeeded, but there were failures.

On one occasion I took him to the plant to meet new people since EVERYBODY loves a puppy. Everything went well until one co-worker walked up behind him and barked like a very large dog! Blade was terrified; I was furious! I was never able to convince that individual that what he had done was not funny. I stopped taking Blade to the power plant just in case he associated the power plant with the bad experience and used other locations to make certain that his encounters with people were more positive.

Blade possessed a striking face with a somewhat sad expression plus huge ears and feet. He captivated everyone who ever saw him. He also possessed the special ability to fall asleep ANYWHERE and usually without any warning. On one of those rare occasions where Hilde lowered her standards and consented to play-fight with Blade on the sofa, Blade fell asleep during the fight! Yep, got it on film. I once saw him just fall over, sigh and start snoring...I almost had heart failure before I realized that he was simply asleep! I spent considerable time placing him in a show pose (stacking) and he was content to remain in that pose even at an early age. Sometimes he would even doze off while stacked...not that the sessions were long.

Slowly his confidence grew and so did he. His body proportions remained excellent throughout his growth period. Hilde had not been so fortunate and had looked so awkward...a fact that we never acknowledged even when we looked at her photos. The changes had been so gradual that we noticed only that her weight and height had increased. Now that we had a comparison, we were stunned by the difference. Blade's head, like all puppies, was large in proportion to the rest of his body. While the head of a male is almost always larger than that of a female, Blade's head remained on the large side as he grew.

In spite of his larger-than-average head size, Blade never used the greater strength which came with it. His sharp puppy teeth NEVER punctured my skin. He went to great lengths to ensure that he never bit one of his human pack members. Was he aware of his great strength or was it part of his somewhat timid demeanor? He did not play as tough as Hilde had and would not bite a rope or tug toy if a human hand was nearby. He would pull as hard or harder than Hilde, but was just extra careful not to harm anyone. Blade would not confront any member of his pack; he knew his place and was content to be at the bottom. He did not require discipline. Unfortunately, Hilde would give him a reminder of her superior status on a regular basis by charging him and knocking his front legs out from under him. She would then stand over him for a few seconds and then depart. On other occasions she just loudly growled at him. Eventually she honed her talent to the point that she could destroy him with just a stare.

As with Hilde, we conditioned him to being touched while eating. We took his food and toys away from him and he simply accepted this as the way things were. No matter what conditions or restrictions we placed on him, he accepted them without protest. I preferred a little more self-confidence, but Blade just would not respond. I secretly hoped to see Blade show at least a little aggression.

Although Blade did not destroy household items, he did demonstrate curiosity toward many items. He usually required only a stern "No" to end the transgression. Often, though, he would do this several times in succession. We had briefly utilized a soda can with five or six pennies inside to correct Hilde and decided to give it a try. I put tape over the opening of the can and waited. Blade decided to check something on the counter and I tossed the can nearby. Blade required two more of these surprises before associating the noise with the bad deed. He did not like that can. In fact, placing the can anywhere would ensure that he avoided that area entirely.

One of my friends who learned that we had acquired another dog asked how much Blade had cost us. I replied, "Twenty-five thousand dollars." He stared at me for a few seconds and asked, "You paid twenty-five thousand dollars for a DOG?" I smiled and said, "Well, he came with a Chevy Blazer." There was no way to haul two dogs in our Saturn coupe and it had been time to trade in my old pickup, anyway. Actually I just needed an excuse to buy a four-wheel drive vehicle. Thanks, Blade.

Chapter 9

Showtime

It had been a long wait. We had expected Hilde to be in the show ring at approximately six months of age, but it was to be ten months longer. Hilde's first show was at a nearby town on a Saturday followed by another show the following day at another relatively close location. Normally we would have delivered Hilde to Sue's kennel for some pre-show tuning up and she would have brought Hilde to the show. Not this time; Sue was vacationing on Cape Cod and it was one of those rare occasions where she would be arriving at a show without several dogs. Another couple was bringing a dog for his show ring debut and we were to meet up with them. "Just look around for another confused couple with a Weimaraner who seem to be searching for someone." That is how we met Sean, Jen and Colby. Colby had never worn a show collar or even been handled as a show dog. Here we were, two couples with two dogs for a dog show and no clue as to what would happen next. We DID know the time for the Weimaraner judging to begin and that time was rapidly approaching with no sign of Sue. Where was she? Should we go check in? What if she doesn't make it...are WE supposed to take the dogs into the ring? Certainly I had no intention of doing so and Sean quickly dismissed the idea also.

We had Blade with us and he was content to simply sleep. Colby and Hilde, however, finished checking each other out and felt the need to extend the practice to every dog passing within range (another reason why shaking hands is preferable to sniffing...humans only shake hands with SOME of the people, not every single one). Actually, politicians seem to emulate the dog method and I certainly intend no disrespect to the dogs!

The afternoon temperature kept climbing as the forecast cloud cover disappeared...good old New England weather. We purchased some bottled water for the dogs rather than rush back to the Blazer and take the chance of missing some of the action. We wanted to stroll through the vendor area just to see what they had to offer, but feared missing Sue's arrival and jeopardizing our first show entry.

Tourist traffic had delayed Sue and she arrived just in time to take Colby for some quick practice prior to entering the ring. We watched as he won his class and then triumphed over the winners from each of the other male classes. None of us understood the significance of those previous events, but we were impressed anyway.

Sue exited the ring with Colby, turned him over to Sean and told him to remain nearby with Colby. She then took Hilde for some quick education and practice prior to her class being called. Sue and Hilde soon entered the ring and I remained near the ring entrance with Sean and Colby while Bobbie relocated to the opposite side of the ring. Bobbie captured all of the action on tape so that later we could watch and learn. At one point Bobbie noticed Sue waving at her and being the extrovert that she is, of course she waved back. Eventually she determined that Sue wanted her to move and promptly did so. Later we found out that there was a good chance that Hilde would see Bobbie or pick up her scent and could react unpredictably during a critical part of the judging. We tried to understand what was happening as each dog was judged individually and as part of the class. We did figure out that Hilde had not won her class; she took fourth place. It was also apparent that Hilde did not enjoy being placed into her show stance (stacked).

Sue directed Sean to keep Colby cooled down with a cold, wet towel and later took him into the ring again for the Best of Breed competition. There he picked up Best of Winners and Best of Breed. Thus his ring debut earned him a first in his class, Winners Dog, Best of Winners and

Best of Breed. None of us understood what any of that meant, but three of the ribbons were nice and the fourth was really impressive! Also, he had earned points toward champion while Hilde had a white ribbon and nothing else. Was the judge blind? Crushed, we left rather than wait for the Sporting Group competition where Colby would be the Weimaraner representative. It was a disappointment issue rather than a sportsmanship issue which we tried to hide under the guise of the afternoon heat. Did we fool anybody...? Tomorrow would be better: a different location and a different judge. Surely that judge would see Hilde as we did.

We departed without being much wiser about the whole process. We did learn, however, that the sight or scent of the owner could affect the actions of the dog in the ring. Mental note: bring ice and a towel tomorrow to cool Hilde down if necessary.

The next day the Weimaraner judging was scheduled in the morning. We arrived early and were soon joined by Sean, Jen and Colby. Colby had not placed in the Group competition, but Sean and Jen were beaming and mentioned how much fun yesterday had been. We lamely agreed. Don't get me wrong, we were glad to see Colby do so well on his first time in the ring. It was just that we had waited so long and the initial results had been so disappointing.

Virtually all of the dogs from the previous show were there for this competition and I think we all expected the same results. Colby picked up a ribbon, but nothing like the previous day. Sue took Hilde into the ring and emerged with a second place ribbon. I assumed our day was over until Sue mentioned that Hilde would go back into the ring if the winner of Hilde's class were to win over all of the other winners of their respective classes. (I know, I had trouble following it also!) She did and Hilde re-entered the ring so that the "second best" or Reserve female could be picked. Hilde took Reserve Winners Bitch which basically meant that if the Winners Bitch could not compete in Best of Breed, Hilde would go in as the representative of all of the females from the various classes. We didn't really understand it, but we loved it! Hilde was finally getting the recognition she deserved.

Sometime during this time Sue asked if I would be interested in taking Hilde into the ring should she be unavailable for any reason. She explained that she could end up with two dogs to show simultaneously and no one to help. I was not interested since I could not follow the action much less be right in the middle of it. She asked me to think about it since Hilde spent part of her time in the ring trying to find us and it could be a disaster if she picked up our scent. We had witnessed such an event where the dog bolted toward the owners sitting next to the ring. The dog cut in front of the handler, tripping her and frightening the dog. No one was injured, but the dog certainly did not have a good time and often it is the dog's attitude that makes it a winner. I told Sue that I would give it some thought.

Bobbie and I discussed it and decided that being able to show Hilde myself would be a prudent choice. My only reservation was the probability of making a fool of myself in front of someone who knew us. We searched for an upcoming show that would be small and at a good distance away in order to minimize the possibility of knowing anyone there. There was a two-day show in Bangor, Maine and if we could make the entry deadline I was willing to try. First things first: the Eastern Futurity/Maturity was two weeks away and Hilde had been entered in the Futurity.

The Eastern Futurity/Maturity was held in Maryland in conjunction with an all-Weimaraner show and we made the drive full of high hopes. This was Hilde's longest trip and she handled it well. We spent two nights in a dog-friendly motel and Hilde had no problem with that. The showgrounds were out in the middle of nowhere and it was surprising to see the various tents set up in a large field. The show from two weeks prior had overwhelmed me with more Weimaraners than I had ever seen, but nothing had prepared me for this sight. There were Weimaraners everywhere and dozens more were still in the vehicles, crates or pens! We had a field day with the camcorder. Hilde did not place in the specialty show, but that did not bother us one bit.

The next day was the Eastern Futurity and we were hoping that Hilde would do well. Sue was unable to take Hilde into the ring due to her other entries and prevailed upon Judy Colan of Colsidex Kennels to do the honors. Sue had known Judy for several years and we suddenly realized that Judy owned Hilde's sire! With Hilde in such good hands we were free to watch the judging and recorded the entire show. When Hilde entered the ring, we stayed out of the wind and out of her view until retrieving her from Judy. Hilde had a fourth place finish and a large ribbon with rosette, a medallion, a bag of dog food and a stuffed toy Weimaraner. We were quite happy, but still didn't understand what had transpired at the show. The drive home was long and it rained, but we didn't mind. Of course, Hilde didn't care...ho hum.

Time flew by and we received our paperwork for the Bangor shows. Off we went to Bangor and it suddenly dawned on me that Hilde had more ring experience than I had. Sue had arranged for another handler to show Hilde the first day and she picked up a red ribbon. The next day I was on my own. Hilde was ready and we arrived very early. Bobbie had the camcorder so that we could critique the performance and make improvements.

There were too many dogs at the ring entrance and I felt that it would be wise to keep Hilde away from them. We adjourned to an isolated area near an entrance door. Hilde was very calm and I was busy mentally running through my responsibilities while Bobbie secretly recorded us. Hilde was preoccupied with stealing and eating treats from a nearby table. A young couple came over to us, petted Hilde and wished us luck. I mentioned that this would be a first for me and they told me to relax and to wave to them when I went past their chairs. "Okay, I can do that."

Finally the big moment came; Hilde and I entered the ring. As a former Navy helicopter pilot I had experienced engine failures, flight control malfunctions and near-midair collisions, but nothing like this! I was primarily concerned with not committing some gross error or breach of etiquette that would somehow shake the AKC to its very core. Of course there were rules concerning conduct of the dog and its handler and I was a walking case of ignorance. So all of this pressure was something that I brought upon myself.

I was in the ring for more than nine minutes and I only remember one thing. When I was stacking Hilde, she decided not to cooperate. As I placed each foot into the desired position, she would move it in sheer defiance. By this time the judge was finished with Hilde's predecessor and turned her attention to Hilde. At that instant everything fell into place and I squatted and steadied Hilde's tail with my left hand and lifted her head with my right. Hilde immediately stepped up onto my right thigh and held her head high...it was magnificent and she knew it! Hilde in all of her glory! The expression on the judge's face was a mixture of pain and disbelief. I was horrified. Then my conscious brain shut down.

I have no recollection of subsequent events until I found myself outside the ring with Hilde's leash in my left hand, a blue ribbon in my pocket and a Reserve Winners ribbon in my right hand. Bobbie congratulated us and I asked her what had happened. She thought that was hilarious; I didn't. The young couple came by and asked why I failed to wave. I did not recall seeing them and they pointed out the only two chairs in the vicinity of the ring. I had passed them four times at a distance of approximately eight feet! I wondered what else I had missed...we all have had those times where we have been so intent on some issue that we performed a series of actions mechanically (driving, walking, etc.) without any recollection of those actions. Usually they are accomplished at a satisfactory level since everything seems fine except for that little wondering of "how did I get here?" This was different...I was not capable of performing my show ring duties mechanically...I did not have any experience to draw upon. On the other hand, I was not bruised, bleeding or otherwise damaged. Since no one was staring, perhaps I had not strayed too far from acceptable levels. And there was no apparent change in Hilde.

I couldn't wait to get home and review the tape just to see what had transpired during my departure from conscious thought. Most of the return trip was spent trying to remember what had happened in the ring and asking Bobbie for the details. After an eternity, we arrived home and I placed the tape in the VCR and sat down to watch the show. I saw Hilde stealing the treats while I concentrated on my upcoming duties followed by a post-ring pose with Hilde and the two ribbons. The segment I wanted was not there. "Honey, did you notice the letters "REC" in the viewfinder when you filmed us IN the ring?" Mental note: explain the difference between "PAUSE" and "REC" when viewed through the viewfinder.

Obviously I had lived through the experience and things could only get better. I could work with Hilde and perhaps we could come to an understanding even if it was just during the time in the ring. I spent more time stacking her in her show stance and she gradually began to accept the placement of her feet as something to be endured. Hilde would never enjoy the show ring, but it would be some time before I would recognize that as a fact.

Chapter 10

Working With Two

We checked with Sue for Hilde's next show and commenced renewed emphasis on Blade's training. He was showing a very smooth and powerful gait and handled very nicely on the leash. When stacked, he stood motionless and seemed not to mind being checked from head to toe. Usually when he stopped, he was in a near-perfect show pose and required very little correction and some times none at all. My experiences with Hilde were starting to pay off. Don't get me wrong, I did not consider myself to be an accomplished handler by any means! Once again we were waiting for the magic six-month point so that he could be shown in the ring.

We began taking both dogs with us to the supermarket. While Bobbie did the grocery shopping, I kept the dogs where they could observe customers entering and leaving the store. This was to let them become more at ease around crowds and become more tolerant of strangers. Many shoppers would stop to observe and sometimes even pet both animals. Children were usually excited when they first saw the dogs; occasionally a few were a little apprehensive. The dogs were uncomfortable at first, but soon warmed up to this new experience. Each successive supermarket session was greeted with increasing enthusiasm by both dogs and their behavior was rapidly becoming a source of pride to both of us. The highlight was when Bobbie exited the supermarket and called their names: Hilde and Blade would go absolutely crazy! At some point in time, they simply accepted the fact that she would emerge and would keep an eye out for her arrival. Luckily, We were able to put the groceries in the back of the Blazer without fear of either dog sampling the goods...another pleasant surprise.

* *

One day Bobbie and I returned home only to be greeted by a very nervous Blade in the unfenced front yard. He was so happy to see us! Hilde was still in the backyard and somewhat frantic or jealous since Blade was loose. We brought him into the house and then out into the backyard. I could find no escape point and both gates were closed. I re-checked the entire fence and still could find no possible exit point. Could he have climbed over the fence? Surely he was not capable of jumping over

The outside area along the fence showed evidence of a frenzied Blade attempting to find his way back into the yard. The destruction was confined to about seventy-five feet along two sides of the yard. Most of the damage was to blueberry plants, raspberry plants and my prize thornless blackberry plants. They would grow back. My immediate concern was to locate his exit point.

I resorted to crawling along the fence and finally spotted something out of place. There was a tennis ball on the hill that slopes down to the little creek behind our house. Blade had recently shown a little interest in the same tennis balls that Hilde loved to play with. Directly up the hill above the tennis ball was a small depression in the yard where the fence did not quite touch the ground; there was perhaps a one-half inch gap. Apparently Blade had attempted to retrieve a tennis ball which had come to rest against the fence at that particular place. During his attempts to grab the ball, he must have pushed it under the fence. Soon he had his head under the fence and eventually must have worked his entire body through the opening. Once outside, he had no real motivation to grab the tennis ball and work his way back inside. I called Blade to me and sure enough, he had some scratches and welts on his side where the fence had scraped. Mystery solved. I repaired the damage to the plants as best I could and commenced fixing the fence although I did not expect Blade to ever try to escape again. Remember the term "imprint?"

While rendering that section of the fence escape-proof, I realized that this must be the same spot where Hilde's snapping turtle had made its entrance. About two months earlier I had discovered a large snapping turtle in our back yard early one morning as I prepared to let Hilde outside. I left Hilde inside and very carefully grabbed the turtle, carried it down to the creek and released it. I had often seen snapping turtles crossing roads and just assumed that this one was simply moving to a new home. Although puzzled as to how the turtle could have entered the yard, I quickly dismissed the incident. Two days later Hilde went out early in the morning and met the same turtle which was digging a hole in which to lay her eggs. Well that explained why the turtle was in the yard. Hilde decided to sniff the turtle and in the process learned why they are called snapping turtles! The resulting scar is still visible. We are certain that Hilde made a mental note to never again sniff a snapping turtle. We re-located the turtle once again and had no more visits from her. When I finished repairing that section of the fence, I knew that neither Blade nor the turtle would be able to crawl under it again.

I was not really worried about Blade escaping and continued working with him to have him ready to show at six months of age. Returning home from work one afternoon I observed a large bump on Blade's head, just above his left eye. It was tender to the touch and his eye was just slightly closed due to the swelling. We were aware of it, watched it and had observed nothing which indicated that it was anything more than a simple bump. Two days later it was even larger. Off to the vet! An x-ray indicated that there was a separation between the main part of the skull and the bone that was forming the bump. The plan was to leave it alone and observe it for the next few days. Sure enough, the swelling decreased although that part of his head never quite returned to its original size. We checked the backyard for anything which might have caused the problem, but never found it. One day I happened to see both dogs rush around to the side yard to check out something. Blade was leading Hilde, but she was rapidly gaining. Just as they approached the kennel, Blade slowed abruptly and Hilde flew past him. He then sped up to join her. I am convinced that the same thing happened earlier and that Hilde overtook Blade and forced him into the steel pipe that forms the corner of the kennel. That would explain both the severity and location of the bruise.

Training with Hilde and Blade continued and usually I was able to work with them right in front of the house. One afternoon while I was working with Hilde, Big Kitty dropped by and sprawled out on the front steps awaiting his evening snack. We finished the training session and headed for the front door. Approaching the steps, Hilde and I spotted the huge cat at the same time. Holding the leash tightly, I allowed Hilde to approach Big Kitty who was now sitting near the front door. Unaware of any previous negative encounters, I hoped that they would sniff each other and perhaps maintain some degree of civility. Nope! Hilde moved abruptly and Big Kitty quickly embedded some rather large claws in Hilde's very tender nose. Hilde withdrew slightly, looking puzzled while Big Kitty simply sat there. We are certain that she made a mental note to add "Large Cats" to her list of Things Not To Sniff. I eased the large feline out of the way and led Hilde into the house where I stopped the blood flow. That done, I put Blade on the leash and CARRIED him out for some practice.

We worked for several minutes and then I let him do a little restricted exploring. On our way back to the front door I was surprised to see Big Kitty sitting there grooming himself and possibly waiting to pass judgment on Blade, too. I knew that Blade had never encountered a cat before and after the episode with Hilde, I was fearful of a repeat performance. I was preparing to pick Blade up and carry him into the house when I decided to let the two meet. Blade slowly eased up to Big Kitty and the large cat gently tapped him on the nose twice with claws retracted. This was done very carefully and apparently as a warning, but it was clear that Blade was not considered a threat. Blade eased back slightly and the two animals stared at each other for a few seconds. Suddenly, Big Kitty resumed grooming himself and I opened the front door. Blade entered the house and that was their first and only contact. A few days later, Big Kitty lost an encounter with a car while crossing the street. I doubt that the two would have been enemies.

We quickly learned that the two dogs would not remain calmly in the back of the Blazer when traveling. Rather, one or both would attempt to migrate to the front seats. We purchased and installed a barrier after folding the rear seats. This provided ample room for the dogs and a crate or crates as necessary. Hilde was already a seasoned traveler and Blade quickly caught on. We took them almost everywhere. A key ingredient in raising dogs is to provide numerous experiences so that the dog learns to accept all kinds of new things without fear.

On one excursion we were traveling along at 55 mph when we heard the rush of air in the back...Hilde had lowered one of the rear windows, stuck her head out and was thoroughly enjoying this forbidden activity! I didn't think she would jump through the window, but it was a very real possibility. I raised the window partially and took control of all windows while maneuvering to the side of the road. She would not respond to any commands to move away from the window. Once we stopped, Hilde moved her head and I closed the window. From then on we tried to remember to put the window control on "lock" if we had the dogs onboard. It was an inconvenience for the person in the front passenger's seat and thus we would "unlock" the window control as necessary. Hilde always tested the window switches right after vehicle entry and this served as our reminder to place the control back into the "locked" position.

A few days later I was reduced to pedestrian status due to a problem with Michael's truck. Bobbie dropped me off at work and returned that afternoon to take me home. She had brought both dogs and had lowered a rear window a few inches so Hilde could see me approach. Bobbie then left the driver's seat, walked around to the passenger's side and re-entered the Blazer. Simultaneously Hilde spotted me and in her excitement, hit the "up" button on the window control. I saw the window move and immediately raced around to the driver's door! There was the very real possibility that the window could cause severe or fatal injury! Bobbie was unable to reach the master switch and could only watch. After what seemed like an eternity, I reached the driver's door and the window controls. Luckily, a startled Hilde had moved her foot off the switch just as the glass touched her neck. She was unable to pull her head back inside, but was not injured. The next day I modified the barrier to prevent access to the rear window switches. At the same time I became aware of the gap between the rear passenger doors and the lowered seat backs.

This was an injury waiting to happen. Armed with some plywood, foam and material similar to that used for plastic seats, I constructed a platform which perfectly followed the contours of the lowered seats and the doors. This was anchored by its unique shape and two holes in the plywood where the vertical supports for the barrier passed through. Luckily, I was able to turn this two-hour project into one requiring eight hours. This was primarily due to my insistence on a perfect fit. The project was successful. And it looked good, too.

It was about this time that I inadvertently started a new game which would become the source of embarrassment for Bobbie and me. Each day when I returned from work both dogs would greet me with a great deal of enthusiasm. Bobbie and I were virtually unable to communicate as Blade and Hilde went to great

73

extremes to gain my exclusive attention. At some point in time I would retire to the bedroom to change clothes and both dogs would race to the bedroom and continue to vie for my attention. On one such occasion, I jokingly said, "Who wants to watch me change clothes?" Blade and Hilde immediately raced to the bedroom! Bobbie and I laughed. This became part of the daily routine. It was only a matter of time until I arrived home from work to find some visitors: Bobbie's favorite aunt and uncle. After visiting for a few minutes, I decided to change clothes. Automatically, I uttered the question, "Who wants to watch me change clothes?" Both dogs set new records enroute to the bedroom. Bobbie's aunt and uncle were speechless as I left the room and the expressions on their faces were priceless. Bobbie was left to explain. I was a little embarrassed, but I had left the room! It seems like they cut their visit a little short that day.

Blade's first show was to be November 23, 1997 just before he reached seven months of age. I would be taking him into the ring since Sue and her handlers had their hands full with other entries. We had taken Blade to Camelot so that he could be "fine tuned" for a few days. We were only able to be there on that one day due to my own schedule and Sue brought him to the show. Blade was so happy to see us and I was given some quick instruction on how to present him so that his best features would stand out. We had plenty of time and I took the opportunity to exercise him and let him see that strange new environment.

The show was held in Springfield, Massachusetts at the same location where the New England Exposition is held. It was an indoor show which created some problems that we had not foreseen. Acoustics were terrible and there was essentially nothing to absorb sound. As individual breeders and handlers folded their collapsible crates, most chose to just let them drop which was resulted in a loud crash. Blade was constantly bombarded by the noise from various directions. If he was watching, there was no problem; however, the "surprises" were having a very pronounced effect on him. Other major distractions came in the form of people who bumped him while moving past. As long as I could keep him in those areas of less congestion he was fine, although the sounds of the crates still seemed to bother him. It was easy to see that his confidence was rapidly waning.

Basically, I tried to distract him and reassure him that he was safe. He appeared to relax somewhat, but was still a little on edge. After what seemed like an eternity, Blade's class was called and we entered the ring. In the ring he was remarkably calm, but he lacked that special attitude that he had shown previously. It was clear that Blade would rather be elsewhere. He managed a fourth place finish in his class which was not bad, but we knew he should have done better. He had stacked well and his movements were smooth. Another handler probably would have achieved better results.

I picked up some additional ring experience and realized that I needed to somehow be more of a calming influence and make sure that he had a good time in the ring. Certainly this first time was not a wonderful experience. Oh well, there would undoubtedly be more opportunities. We were both learning.

Somewhere around this time Blade saw his first standard Poodle which was immaculately groomed. Blade was uneasy yet curious. I had been the same way, but I got over it; Blade hasn't.

Chapter 11

Blade Takes Off

The next dog show was located in Worcester, Massachusetts which was near enough that we could drive both days. It was another indoor show and we could only hope that Blade would find it less stressful. He was entered in the six-to-nine-month puppy class and we were expecting better than a fourth place finish.

Saturday he took first in his class, but progressed no further. We were elated yet surprised since he still was not comfortable with the indoor environment. We used some of the extra time to let him explore and he began to accept the noise. He did not object to being touched or bumped as long as he could see it coming. I did my best to prevent anyone from walking up behind him and bumping or petting him, but on those occasions where I failed, I could see an immediate loss of confidence. I learned that no matter how elaborate your blocking or obstructing method, a determined individual will go out of their way to somehow go through this forbidden space rather that walk unopposed through an area as big as a house!

The next day was a repeat of the previous day with one exception: no one surprised him prior to entering the ring. He looked great and was just absolutely perfect! He took first in his class and everything was looking good for Winners Dog. While awaiting the judging of the other male classes, I relaxed my vigil and someone slipped behind him and bumped him. Instantly he reverted to his cautious and nervous state. When we entered the ring for Winners Dog, he was ready to go home. He looked good and handled well, but just didn't have that special spark. That "I'm the best dog here" attitude wasn't there. Needless to say, he did not take Winners Dog.

Hilde had been shown both days with less than spectacular results. There was one incident that was yet another reminder to remain alert with a dog on leash. Hilde took advantage of an opportunity to sniff the butt of a male Rottweiler who was unaware of her presence. I saw the blunder just as it occurred, but did not have time to react. The Rottweiler whirled around and only her quick reflexes saved Hilde from serious injury. The Rottweiler quickly relaxed while Hilde maintained her new position right at my side. The owner of the Rottweiler had been engaged in conversation with two individuals and the sudden lunge by her dog had almost dislocated her shoulder. She was initially angry with me, but quickly realized that she was also partially to blame. Hilde continues to have a VERY healthy respect for Rottweilers!

The next show was the following week at Boston's Bayside Exposition Center. This was a huge four-day show with more than 3,000 entrants from the various breeds. We had both Blade and Hilde entered on the last three days. Hilde won her class each day which was a major morale builder for us. Unfortunately, she did not progress beyond her class. Hilde was shown by Sue each day which took the pressure off me. I was free to concentrate on Blade.

Blade was a different story. His brother/littermate, Frankie, was in the same class and was being shown by Sue, his owner. I was showing Blade and the intimidation factor was quite high. This was the first time that I had competed against Sue although we were not actually competing against each other. I had listened to some of her critiques to handlers who had committed errors with her dogs in the ring. I did not want to be on the receiving end of her method of constructive criticism! This was very serious business to her whereas it was just another learning experience for me. Blade finished second on the first two days with Frankie taking first both times as well as Best of Breed Puppy on Saturday. I couldn't complain about that and I had only received minor and well-deserved criticism from Sue. Things were going well. Seeing Frankie and Blade in a first and second place finish two days in a row validated our view that the four males in that litter had been essentially equal or near-equal. No wonder that picking a puppy had been so difficult.

On the third day I was resigned to the probability of a repeat of the past two days. Surprise! This time the entrants were called in catalogue order and Blade and I entered the ring first since he had the lowest number. This was a new experience for me since Blade and I were "leading the pack" and Blade had never been in this position before. One big advantage was the extra time to set Blade up in his show stance plus the psychological advantage of being in the "first place" position in the lineup. Blade stopped in a perfect pose and the judge got a nice long look at him while the other dogs were still filing in and setting up.

The judge scanned the line of entrants and walked back toward us. Anticipating her direction to "take them around," I gathered Blade's leash and released him from his stance. She then turned and examined the "lineup" again with Blade all set to move out! In absolute horror I furiously tried to stack Blade as the judge approached.

Blade sensed my nervousness and would not respond...I could NOT get him into position and he was standing at a forty-five degree angle to the rest of the dogs! The judge walked up, placed a hand under his chin and asked, "What's the matter, boy?" Blade looked her in the eyes and gave a soft whine as I watched any hope of him even placing evaporate. "Sorry, I guess I jumped the gun a little bit," I stammered. She smiled and told me to "take them around" and where to set up for the "hands on" inspection.

That mistake really took the pressure off me and my concern was just to try to maintain some semblance of dignity until we could exit the ring. I led the pack around to the designated area and set Blade up as the judge watched. Naturally, Blade stacked very nicely and the hands-on inspection was essentially perfect. The "down and back" and the individual "go around" were flawless and soon I could exit the ring and just forget that this ever happened. Please, just don't let me fall down! Newspaper headlines flashed through my mind: "Man Dies in Dog Show Ring After Screwing Up." This was accompanied by "Wife Appalled at Husband's Poor Performance" and "Breeder Disavows Any Association With Klutzy Handler." At least I DID learn another lesson: don't anticipate what the judge will do, but be ready for anything.

After what seemed like an eternity, the judge finished examining the rest of the class and changed the positions of three dogs, but left Blade in front. Looking me straight in the eye and without giving any clues, she said, "Okay, take them around."

I made certain that everyone was ready to go and moved off with Blade, hoping to just survive the "go around." Halfway around the ring she pointed at Blade and said, "First" and continued with second through fourth places. In utter disbelief, I turned around and looked at the handler behind me who said, "Congratulations." I collected the ribbon in a daze...a very happy daze and realized that Blade had won over Frankie. The "congratulations" from Sue was the icing on the cake. Blade did not take Winners Dog, but we didn't care. And there would be no newspaper headlines! Suddenly life was good again.

But there was more to come. After the female puppy classes were judged, Blade went up against the winner and was awarded Best of Breed Puppy. This meant that he would be going up against the other Best of Breed puppies in the Sporting Group later in the afternoon. Sue volunteered to take him into the ring, but since she had a long drive with several dogs I told her that I would be happy to give it a try. Neither of us really expected Blade to win the Group and move up to the Best in Show Puppy competition.

It was several hours until the Group competition and

we had no strategy other than to kill time by checking the various exhibits and maybe putting both dogs in the Blazer for some rest. We walked around with the dogs and they seemed to adapt very well to the loud, crowded indoor environment. During the course of our wanderings we noticed that many of the visitors were children who were anxious to pet some of the hundreds of dogs. In most cases they were forbidden to do so by owners and handlers for various reasons. Those dogs with long coats that required major grooming and those dogs whose judging was imminent were, understandably, off-limits. Unfortunately, the children did not understand and at some point in time their parents just gave up and stopped asking for permission.

While deciding our next course of action, we noticed a couple with two young children who were looking at Blade and Hilde and apparently asked if they could pet the doggies. The parents looked our way and apparently told the two kids to keep walking. The look on their faces proved to be too much...we motioned them over. The kids, a girl about six years old and a boy about four, looked like they must have looked on a Christmas morning! Blade and Hilde welcomed both children and were exceptionally gentle. Even mom and dad got into the action. It was obvious that both kids had eaten various messy things and part of Blade and Hilde's "kisses" were actually taste tests of the food available at the show. The conditioning of our two dogs to being touched was certainly paying off. We were concerned and especially watchful, but the dogs were enjoying the attention and certainly did not consider the kids a threat. We chatted for a few minutes and after profusely thanking us, the young family moved on. After a few steps, the little girl turned around and waved good bye to the dogs. It was a wonderful feeling that something so simple could bring that much joy to those kids.

The big surprise was yet to come...there had been many witnesses to the petting episode and suddenly we had a crowd of people whose children wanted to pet the

"Sesame Street" dogs. The situation bordered on chaos since we were encircled by the crowd. We were forced to make certain that the kids approached from just one direction and that the parents kept their children under control. The kids just wanted to pet the dogs, but the parents wanted to know what breed they were. There were countless questions regarding the breed plus the good and bad points. It must have taken half an hour to eliminate the crowd before we could resume our exploring. Ironically, we all had a good time.

That episode pointed out a need for some sort of a "greet and pet" area at a dog show. It was extremely rewarding and there were no bad experiences on either the human or canine side. We did notice that all of the children and most of the adults did not know how to properly approach a dog. This fact was something that would surface again at a later date.

Eventually, it was time to assemble near the designated show ring for the Sporting Group puppy judging. More than twenty puppies representing their respective breeds were all set to enter the ring when the unexpected happened: the fire alarm went off! Immediate instructions to evacuate the building came over the public address system. We headed for the nearest exit amidst an extremely loud and obnoxious fire alarm klaxon. Both dogs were excited, but were relatively calm considering the noise. Once outside we waited patiently, having seen no indication of a fire. Approximately ten minutes went by before we were cleared to re-enter the building. Unfortunately, the klaxon continued to blast and while Hilde took it all in stride, Blade showed a definite preference to remain outside. We approached the show ring area, the klaxon ceased and the announcer immediately called for the Sporting Group to enter the ring. That announcement really got Blade's attention and he decided that it was definitely time to go home rather than enter the ring. I was stronger and thus we were seventh or eighth to enter the ring.

The crowd was engaged in either applauding, yelling or whistling...which seemed to be even more unsettling to Blade. The Weimaraner judging is usually accompanied by quiet, polite applause...certainly nothing like that which we were experiencing. We stopped with all dogs set up for the judge's first look. I tried calming Blade, but he just wanted out of that place. Then one more surprise: two young girls both sitting just outside the ring decided to kick the portable fencing and that was enough to convince Blade that it was definitely time to go! I was not able to get him back in line, but at least two other nearby handlers had the same problem with their dogs. The girls laughed; we didn't.

As the individual judging took place, the crowd divided into two groups: those with polite applause and those fanatics who yelled, screamed and whistled during the "down and back" and the "go around." What little confidence Blade had retained quickly evaporated. Come on, Blade, just hang in there a few more minutes.

When it was Blade's turn, he stacked surprisingly well. He was adjusting to the crowd noises and, maybe, just maybe, he would be okay. As the judge approached, he was fine. The judge allowed Blade to sniff her hand and commenced her inspection of his head. So far, so good. Then out of the clear blue she said, "Open his mouth." That was a first for me and it was also a first for Blade. I tried to ease his mouth open while saying, "Open." Unfortunately, Blade said, "No!" The judge then attempted to assist and Blade pulled back and practically sat down. It was clear that Blade was not going to cooperate. The change in the judge was immediate; she finished the rest of the "hands on" inspection in about five seconds and sent us on the "down and back" followed by the "go around." The polite applause of the crowd without other noise confirmed what the quick inspection had signaled...Blade would not be advancing! After all dogs had been individually judged, we had one more "go around" and she pulled her choices and excused the rest of us. So much for our first Group experience. A very tired and very happy Blade left the building.

Both dogs had won their classes and Blade had been Best of Breed Puppy so it was a good day although quite long. The next week Blade would gladly open his mouth on command and, of course, that was never again required.

Chapter 12

Picking Up The Pace

We entered both Blade and Hilde in most shows within a 300-mile radius and spent numerous weekends on the road. On the longer trips we would stay at pet-friendly hotels or motels. Some were restrictive on dog size while others simply required that the dogs be crated if left alone in the room. This was usually discussed while making the reservations. We were surprised at the number of reservation clerks who did not know what a Weimaraner looked like and we usually described them as the type of dogs in "such and such" commercial or as "Sesame Street" dogs. That usually provided instantaneous recognition and was often enough to gain approval even if Weimaraners were not on the "approved" list.

Both dogs usually entered the lobby as part of check-in and were invariably well received by the hotel/motel staff. This seemed preferable to bringing in the dogs via other entrances which might be misconstrued by other guests as sneaking in the dogs. Both dogs would stand on their hind legs at the counter and look the clerks right in the eyes, seeming to enjoy this special game. There was never an occurrence where the staff personnel were uncomfortable with Hilde and Blade and the dogs' manners usually generated praise. Occasionally, other hotel/motel occupants would register or feign surprise to learn that dogs were accepted as guests, but we never heard any specific negative comments. No damage, no accidents and many new friends would describe their hotel visits. Neither dog would bark unless there was a knock at the door.

One group of Japanese tourists was clearly surprised

when their elevator doors opened to reveal Hilde and Blade waiting to enter. After the initial surprise, most were eager to pet the dogs and language problems were overcome by universal gestures. Cameras appeared from nowhere and the posing began. Everyone enjoyed the experience with Hilde and "Brade" and I suppose that you could consider them to have been international goodwill ambassadors.

One great thing about Weimaraners is that they are "wash and wear" dogs. Bathing them was easy and rather than gamble with possible skin problems, we always used Neutrogena shampoo and conditioner. We never experienced any problems. Blow drying was not really necessary if a large towel was utilized. Both dogs loved the toweling process. Blade would go crazy after smelling the conditioner residue on Hilde and would chase her through the house. Perhaps he associated that fragrance with another road trip and was just eager to go.

We had initially used the guillotine-type nail clippers when trimming their nails, but as the dogs grew larger neither dog appreciated the intense pressure that was required. We accidentally stumbled upon a small portable grinder that was rechargeable. It came with a small sanding drum and seemed like a perfect solution. Hilde was the test case and did not object to the process. The buzzing sound caught her attention, but she got over it in a hurry. Blade quickly adapted to the new process, but was always wary of the grinder. The process was quick, easy and certainly less traumatic for the dogs. It was also much easier on me.

At one show we roamed the commercial exhibitors area just to see what items were for sale. Of course there were exhibits by the major dog food companies. There were also all types of treats and snacks plus collars, leashes and all manner of grooming aids. There was also a huge selection of toys; many were unlike any we had ever seen in stores. One particular item in the toy category caught our eye: two tennis balls connected by a short rope. We immediately thought of Hilde and decided to purchase one. Then we thought of Blade and purchased a second one. Maybe the two dogs would engage in some tug of war games. The darn things cost $11 each, but it was a small price for things certain to bring joy to the two dogs. We waited until we arrived home and had unloaded everything from the Blazer and then gave the toys to the dogs. Blade raced away to our bedroom and returned in a few minutes with one of the tennis balls. He was so happy...he had fixed the problem with the tennis ball by removing the rope. We were shocked and utterly speechless and Blade quickly disappeared. Soon he was back with the OTHER tennis ball and no rope attached to that one either! He was strutting around and wagging his tail waiting for the praise that he deserved. Bobbie mumbled something about eleven dollars flying out the window. Within thirty minutes Blade had seized Hilde's toy and reduced it to three separate parts, also. This time Bobbie mentioned something about twenty-two dollars and something to do with a toilet. We only purchased regular tennis balls after that.

As Blade grew, he slowly began to become more assertive...not more aggressive. He worked hard at crawling under the fence to visit Bailey next door. The three dogs would bark playfully at each other and that would cause Blade to renew his efforts to crawl under the fence. His initial escape months before had indeed been imprinted and he would continue this behavior. He destroyed (and I mean DESTROYED) one section of the common chainlink fence and I reinforced that area with chicken wire. Soon I was forced to anchor some heavier wire fencing in the ground adjacent to the entire fenceline to prevent him from digging under it. This fencing was then tied to the chainlink fence and he attacked that! The new electric fence wire at the base of the chainlink fence solved the problem, but only after two more escapes. Finally we could breathe easier...at least for awhile. Unknown to me, the grounded side of the electric fence was not sufficient to guarantee a reliable "shock" every time. Hilde could sense the operation of the fence by approaching it carefully while Blade would periodically check it physically. After observing his avoidance of the fence for several weeks, I unplugged the fence charger. Perhaps he would no longer test the fence. Silly me.

Blade was winning his class on a regular basis while Hilde was picking up second or third place finishes. Finally the Eastern Futurity/Maturity arrived and was part of a four-day collection of shows. The first was exclusively Weimaraners and Blade took a third in his class while Hilde failed to place. The second show was the Futurity/Maturity and Blade took First Place Junior Dog! We were ecstatic! Hilde failed to place in the Maturity, but we were not expecting her to do so. The third show provided Blade with a third place in his class while Hilde picked up a second place finish. The fourth show saw Hilde pick up a fourth place and Blade won first in his class, Winners Dog and Best of Winners. He had won his first points toward champion!

Since they were competing against basically the same dogs each day, the variations in placements were surprising to me. Each judge interprets the breed standard differently and some have distinct preferences for certain types of dogs. Admitted, they also perform a "hands on" inspection which provides additional information that mere observers do not receive. The attitude of the dog also plays a tremendous role and that is something which is not a "given" from day to day.

Less than a month later, a Saturday show provided Hilde with a fourth place finish in her class. Blade won his class, took Winners Dog, Best of Winners and finally, Best of Breed. In the Sporting Group competition he managed a third place finish...it was a VERY good day and more points toward champion! The following day Blade won his class and then took Winners Dog and picked up more points. Hilde also gave us a surprise.

Keep in mind that Hilde simply did not care for dog

shows...she just went there to sniff the other dogs. I took her into the ring without hope for much more than another fourth place finish since she was competing with the same entrants from the previous day. Everything was normal until the judge approached for the "hands on" inspection. Hilde typically required a large amount of pressure to keep her head up. The judge spoke to her and offered her hand for Hilde to sniff. Almost immediately Hilde relaxed and the judge continued checking the head and mouth. She then continued with the neck, shoulders and along Hilde's back. I was not prepared for what happened next. I had my hand under Hilde's jaw and suddenly she lifted her head and tilted it up and back until she was staring at the judge. I heard several gasps (one must have been mine!) and I heard someone say, "Look at that!" The judge looked up and saw Hilde's upsidedown head (and probably my dumbfounded expression). "What a sweet girl," she said with a smile. I mumbled something about her never doing THAT before and waited for the axe to fall. Nothing. She completed her inspection and sent us on the "down and back" and the "go around." Shortly thereafter, she awarded Hilde second place. We left the ring and the other class winners entered the ring for Winners Bitch. The first place winner from Hilde's class took Winners Bitch so Hilde and I re-entered the ring for Reserve Winners Bitch. The judge looked over the assemblage and re-checked one or two, smiled, pointed at Hilde and said "Reserve." With a huge smile she handed the ribbon to me and said, "Congratulations." I said, "There's something about you that she really likes." I guess it was my way of apologizing for Hilde's lack of decorum. In retrospect, I wish I could have seen it from a spectator's point of view! There is no doubt in my mind that the episode gave Hilde the Reserve spot.

Bobbie and I had always been hungry by the time that we finished each show. Since we usually had a long drive ahead of us, we often sought out a fast food restaurant along our route. Most of the time we chose the first available restaurant. For some unknown reason we made a pact with the dogs: do well and it's Wendy's; otherwise, it's McDonald's. This was actually our way of letting other things dictate our stopping point and it made the whole process more random. Of course the dogs ended up with a plain hamburger in either case. When ordering a plain (really plain) hamburger, never mention that it is for the dogs...some people are offended by that!

Hilde picked up three more second place finishes and one more third place before retiring from ring competition. She would go on to other successes in the months to come, but they would not be in the ring. She would be allowed to follow her instincts.

Sue had reminded us of the need to have Hilde's hips x-rayed as part of the Orthopedic Foundation of America (OFA) certification. This was in preparation for the first of two required breedings as part of the co-ownership agreement. She preferred that we utilize her vet since her vet had considerable expertise in this area and we agreed. We took Hilde to the vet and picked her up while she was still a little unsteady from the sedative used to make the process a little easier. A few days later it was time for her annual booster inoculations and we took her to our own vet. Hilde had always loved Dr. Newman and had absolutely no fear of the vet's office. When it was time for her first shot, we received quite a shock. I held Hilde while she stood on the examining table and Dr. Newman prepared the syringe. There was no cause for concern...Hilde always endured these things with no reaction whatsoever. As soon as she felt the needle, she yelped, spun around and showed the vet her extensive dental array. The syringe bounced off the wall and the room became extremely quiet. Dr. Newman said to Hilde, "It's okay" and to me, "Did she recently have her hips x-rayed?"

Well I was impressed! While preparing another syringe, he explained that a sedative is normally used to keep the dog sufficiently calm to stay steady while the x-ray is taken. The dog is alert enough to realize that it is extremely vulnerable and yet can do nothing about it. This condition is remembered and the dog may take steps to prevent it from happening again. We were extremely alert during the subsequent injection and no problems were encountered. Hilde no longer likes Dr. Newman or his office.

Things were relatively quiet for a few weeks until I received a phone call at work from a near-hysterical Bobbie. She had returned home from an errand and Blade was missing! Since he did not wander far from the yard if he escaped, someone must have stolen him. The locks were on both gates and Blade was not one to jump over the fence. Bobbie had repeatedly called his name to no avail and checked everywhere, but could not find him. She asked me to come home which was a given, anyway. I envisioned everything from stolen to stuck by a vehicle. "Contact all of the local veterinarians." I tried to sound calm, but my heart was pounding and my mind was racing!

Leaving work, I formulated a quick search of the neighborhood even though I knew Blade would not wander far if he had actually escaped. I checked various side streets and open areas near the house, but saw no trace of him. With heavy heart and the knowledge that Bobbie would somehow blame herself for his absence, I pulled into the driveway and rushed to the house.

I opened the front door and was greeted by a very excited Blade and a very tearful Bobbie! When I could finally understand her words interspersed with the sobs of joy, I learned that he had escaped again. A neighbor had caught him once as a young puppy escapee and had been able to lift him over the fence. Luckily the same neighbor had spotted Blade this time and easily collared him. The gates were locked, no one was home and Blade was now far too heavy to be lifted over the fence. Rather than just leave him outside, the neighbor had taken him home and allowed him into his enclosed porch area while watching for one of us to arrive home.

Shortly after Bobbie phoned me, she went out into the front yard to call Blade. Suddenly, the neighbor yelled that he had something that she was probably looking for. It was Blade! He said that he would just turn Blade loose since he thought Blade would go straight home. And Blade DID go straight home (through briars, shrubs and oblivious to any possible vehicular traffic) to a joyous reunion!

We presented our neighbor with a gift certificate to a local restaurant as a small token of our gratitude. He tried to decline it stating that his actions were "the neighborly thing to do." He felt guilty accepting the gift certificate and we felt guilty for placing such a small value on Blade's safe return.

An inspection of the yard revealed that Blade had not attempted to go visit Bailey next door; neither had he observed something in the street or front yard which caused him to attempt an escape at that point. He picked an area in the back yard that was the only possible area for him to exit. He must have tested numerous areas and somehow determined that the one area was vulnerable. He quickly learned that the electric wire was not "hot" and proceeded to demolish the chain link fence and the back-up wire fencing. His determination to escape was rewarded, but he was unable to return via the same route. He had remained in the front yard waiting for someone to open the gate and allow him back into the yard. Luckily, his barking had attracted the attention of our neighbor.

I installed three grounding rods for the electric fence and re-connected the fence charger. Blade checked it that night and was convinced that it was now something to be avoided. That was his last escape, at least for a while. Since that particular escape mode had been imprinted, it was only a matter of time until he made another attempt to crawl under the fence.

Chapter 13

Blade Begins to Move

Blade picked up another first and Winners Dog, repeated that at the next show and then had several shows where he just couldn't seem to even win his class. At outdoor shows he was superb; indoor shows were always an unknown. An incident occurred during this time which showed the importance of the dog's attitude.

I was warming him up for one of his indoor shows and had been pleasantly surprised by his attitude. As usual, we had arrived early and had plenty of time before his class was to be called. I was able to stack him and gait him several times and it was obvious that he was absolutely enjoying himself. He was exceptionally alert and confident and was receiving many admiring glances and comments from spectators who were milling around. He did look great. Since we still had plenty of time and since he was doing so well, I decided to take him exploring. We worked our way through the crowd and everything was fine until we passed a group of German Shepherds awaiting their entrance into the ring. They were on my right as we passed and Blade, naturally, was on my left. There were no problems until we retraced our path.

I was still marveling over Blade's confident attitude and was congratulating myself on the decision to take him exploring. I do not actually recall approaching the German Shepherds, but I had obviously dropped my guard. All of a sudden, a large male growled and lunged at Blade! He was being held by a boy about ten years of age who was no match for the big dog's strength. Blade immediately pulled back and suddenly I was between the two dogs. Instinctively I tried to protect Blade without thinking of the possible consequences. Luckily someone grabbed the Shepherd and restrained him. I was able to ease Blade past the larger dog and into an open area. I do not know what triggered the incident, but it was a reminder to always be alert for the unexpected. Those few seconds brought about a major change in Blade.

Gone was the confidence and poise. He began constantly checking the surrounding area, tail down and head lowered. I tried gaiting him, but he would not carry his head and tail as he had done just minutes prior to the incident. I tried distracting him with treats and different locations but to no avail. There was some eventual improvement though not enough for him to even win his class...the spark just wasn't there. Blade still does not care for German Shepherds.

* * * * * * * * * * * * * * * * * * * *

By this time we had collected more and more items to pack along for the various shows. Previously we had only required a show collar and leash plus some multi-purpose wipes. As the weather became warmer, at outdoor shows we needed ice for cooling and even purchased a small tent for shade at those locations where there were no trees. Earlier we had tried to keep the dogs under the tent near the entrance to the designated ring entrance, but the crowd and other dogs just created too many other problems. We used the tent once...it was too hot. We then resorted to towels dipped in cold water. That worked, but both dogs preferred something less drastic. More water with less ice was acceptable to all.

Blade's slump continued for several shows. Then, just as quickly, he won his class, Winners Dog and Best of Winners. His confidence had returned. Three weeks later he picked up a second place and Reserve Winners Dog. The next show provided him with a first in class, Winners Dog and Best of Winners. The next show gave him another first in class and Reserve Winners Dog. He repeated the results the next day. We went to Troy, New York and he won his class, Winners Dog and Best of Winners. He needed one more point for champion. The following day he won his class and took Reserve Winners Dog. He still needed one more point.

Prior to one of the previous shows I had racked my brain trying to think of something that would make Blade a true standout at one critical point of his judging. At the conclusion of the "down and back" the handler stops the dog just prior to reaching the judge. The handler then steps away from the dog and in theory the dog assumes a perfect, natural pose without being touched by the handler. Small food tidbits (also known as "bait") or a special toy may also be held up and the end result is a very alert and striking exhibition of what the dog can look like at its very best...at least that is the hoped-for result.

Blade always looked good at that point, but would often yawn at the critical time. If only I could find something special that would get his attention. Blade did not respond well to any type of food as bait. There was no special toy that would work. While exercising him near a local cranberry bog, I noticed a feather from a Canadian goose. I grabbed it and hid it from Blade. I stacked him and then did a "down and back." I brought him to a stop, stepped away and showed the feather to him. Wow! His ears were raised slightly and his gaze was fixed on the feather. The transformation was breathtaking...I had the answer!

I worked him a little more and received the same incredible results. I teased him with the feather and then took him home and returned to look for more feathers. I collected several and placed them into a re-sealable plastic bag. Blade's next show was several days away and I was not willing to take the risk of being unable to find more feathers right before the show.

The big day came and I would be taking Blade into the ring since Sue was not available. Armed with my secret weapon, I entered the ring with Blade at my side. It was an outdoor show, the kind that Blade enjoyed the most.

He was relaxed and looked great. There were two other dogs in his class and I was certain that he had the edge over one and possibly both. But I had a secret weapon! The judge completed the "hands on" inspection and Blade was his normal, carefree self. It was now time for the down and back. I turned Blade in front of the judge and moved out smartly; Blade eased in to his best gait and all was well. At the appropriate point, we turned and headed back toward the judge. I reached into my right coat pocket and removed the feather. Just prior to reaching the judge, I stopped Blade and eased ahead of him and let the leash go slack. The judge moved slightly for a better viewing angle and I raised the feather just to the right of my head.

Blade's legs were perfectly positioned and his ears raised slightly as he spotted the feather. Wow, this was perfect! Without warning he leaped at the feather with all four feet leaving the ground! My only reaction was to move the feather. Blade was now in front of me in a not-so-flattering pose with ears raised while he searched for that feather. Still in shock, I heard the judge (who had moved several feet) say, "Well THAT was impressive!" The following silence seemed endless until eventually the judge told me to take him around. Blade won his class and went on to win Reserve Winners Dog, but the judge chose not to send us on the "down and back" again! I dumped the secret weapon...it was too dangerous!

After the show, we went back to our motel and changed into more comfortable clothes. I took Blade out just in case he had to "go" and while walking along a brushy area, Blade slammed into a perfect and very striking point. This was the first time that I had seen Blade point...at least with any intensity. I was flabbergasted. I wasn't able to determine what he had seen or scented, but it certainly brought out something that I had not expected from Blade. Was it a fluke or did his hunting instincts suddenly kick in? I briefly considered the possibility that Blade might be a candidate for some hunt training, but dismissed the idea since I had no idea where to start.

Finally, needing only one more point for Champion, Blade entered the ring at Flushing, New York. With Sue as handler, he won his class, Winners Dog, Best of Winners and Best of Breed. He did not place in the subsequent Sporting Group competition, but we did not care! Champion Camelot's Cutting Edge...it sounded really good. Blade had amassed sixteen points for his champion status rather than the required fifteen. I had shown him when he acquired four of those points and was able to feel that I had made some contribution to the process.

We had no intentions of further show entries for awhile. It was like taking a vacation and winter was coming. Holidays and bad weather would be dictating our routine for the next several weeks and would be a welcome replacement for the harried dog show schedule. A few weeks later we were to undergo a frightening experience.

The calendar rolled over to 1999 and winter had been relatively mild. There had been some snow which Hilde always found to be exhilarating, but Blade regarded snow as something to be endured. In mid-February a blizzard hit around noon and continued through the afternoon. The roads were in terrible shape and even the short trip home from the power plant was treacherous. Upon arrival, I noticed that Michael's girlfriend, Shannon, was there and both dogs were out playing in the snow.

Bobbie and I are movie fiends and I mentioned that this might be an excellent time to catch a movie since there would be no crowds. She would have no part of it and questioned my sanity, citing the roads and the continuing snowfall. I was looking forward to the chance to go out...I had been cooped up inside all day at work and the absence of a window in my office area made things even worse.

Both dogs had been playing in the snow and failed to greet me as they had always done before. This was odd...Blade was just not particularly fond of the snow.

Suddenly they both decided it was time to come inside and we opened the backdoor. We went through the ritual of wiping their feet and then had the "welcome home" celebration. Then both dogs disappeared while Bobbie and I began discussing the events of the day.

Suddenly Shannon shouted, "Something's wrong with Blade!" Bobbie ran to our bedroom and observed Blade standing with his legs spread and fighting to maintain his balance. Michael and I followed and by then Blade was lying on his side with all four legs stretched out straight and rigid. He was not responsive to touch or sound; his eyes were fixed and he was trembling. "Call the vet!" Bobbie rushed to the phone. I asked Shannon what she had seen and she said that she had noticed Blade standing on the bed and unresponsive to her voice and then suddenly he was on his side. Both his pulse and respiration were higher than normal. He also suffered a minor loss of control of bowels and bladder. "The vet's office is closed!" Naturally, it's only two miles away. "Call someone else!"

Bobbie finally reached a vet about ten miles away who was trying to close early because of the storm, but would wait for us. I carried Blade out to the Blazer and we were on our way in minutes. It was too dangerous to go to a movie, but here we were on a record-breaking trip to the vet in a blizzard! There was little traffic...only idiots were out driving. Snowplows were not even out clearing the roads...at least not the roads we were traveling. We did not consider ourselves in the idiot category; we were taking a sick dog...no, a member of our family, to the vet. I tried to balance driving speed with the road conditions and the urgency of his condition. I was pushing my own limits and concentrating on the driving.

Bobbie kept her eyes on Blade and spoke to him in a calm, soothing manner even though she was terrified by his condition. Although groggy at first, Blade appeared to be improving. I was not really much of a comfort to Bobbie...the driving was taking most of my concentration. The first part of the trip was a two-lane highway and there were no vehicles going our way; the one traffic light even cooperated by turning green as we approached. The four lane, divided highway was extremely slushy and I took the left lane almost immediately because of the conditions. The road was hazardous, but staying in the ruts was not too bad. I did not want to change lanes any more than necessary because of the slush. The heavy snowfall continued all the way to the vet's office. The last two miles were two lane with a thirty mile per hour speed limit and we could not maintain much more than twenty mph due to the accumulated snow.

Blade emptied his stomach contents sometime during the drive (I'm certain that it wasn't because of my driving) and seemed to be fine. He was wagging his tail when I opened the tailgate of the Blazer. I was totally exhausted, both physically and mentally when we finally reached the parking lot. I eased him down onto the snow and led him to the vet's office. He appeared perfectly normal.

The vet examined him, drew some blood and ran some other tests. She asked what his activities had been immediately prior to his episode and Bobbie explained that he had been outside playing in the snow for a long period of time. She then asked when he had last eaten and was informed that it had been about seven that morning.

The vet could find nothing wrong and came up with two conclusions: either a seizure or hypoglycemia. She stated that Blade had essentially no excess body fat and probably had used up all of his blood sugar while playing and as a result of his body's attempt to maintain its warmth. She was reluctant to classify the episode as a seizure since our observations were not consistent with those of classic seizure symptoms. She sent us home with directions to keep him under close observation and not to allow him any extended play outdoors.

We were elated about the diagnosis that she favored, but a little nervous about the other possibility. The drive home was slower, safer and certainly more relaxed. Michael and Shannon met us at the door and watched a perfectly normal Blade walk inside. They were really impressed that the vet could produce such incredible results in such a short time!

We watched Blade like hawks for the new few days and were extremely observant when he went outside. We provided snacks throughout the day to keep his blood sugar levels more constant. We waited for a second episode, but it did not come – at least not for awhile.

Chapter 14

The Breeding

It was time to discuss another requirement of the co-ownership arrangement with our breeder, Sue Thomas. Hilde was to provide two litters sired by the male of Sue's choice. Hilde would be reaching her next heat cycle in February and we knew that Hilde would be going to Camelot for a few days for the breeding. It was not a big deal for us, although the thought of the birth of the litter was exciting...but that was several months down the road. We were intent on keeping Hilde's weight at optimum and observing her for the first signs of estrus. Sue indicated that she would be out of the country for a few days, but should be back well prior to Hilde's breeding dates.

We had taken Hilde to Sue's vet for her Orthopedic Foundation of America (OFA) hip x-rays earlier and the final results had come back as "good." This meant that she was acceptable to the American Kennel Club as a breeding female. There were no more obstacles; Hilde was all set. Would her offspring possess most of her traits or those of the sire? The wait began...a common theme when Hilde was involved.

We finally observed first indications of Hilde's upcoming heat cycle and phoned Sue so that she could make preparations as necessary. Surprise, her husband had suffered a severe skiing injury and required considerable care...would we be interested in conducting the breeding? Initially, that was a little absurd...worrying about the male AND the female? Where would the breeding take place? Which male and where was he located? The process had suddenly gone completely out of control. Then she explained that Blade appeared to be an excellent choice for the sire. We agreed, of course, and immediately felt that the breeding would now be relatively easy. Blade's preliminary OFA results were back and his hips were considered "excellent." Everything was looking good. Now it was simply a matter of timing.

The thought of conducting or controlling the breeding was not a big deal. I had grown up on a farm and nature always finds a way, so how could there possibly be any difficulty! We grabbed our copy of *Weimaraner Ways* and read up on the breeding process. One area of concern is that the female often just does not prefer the company of her selected suitor and would prefer to make her own choice. Consequently, that male may receive the wrath of a very angry and unwilling female! Choosing her own mate is usually out of the question in most situations, but sometimes exceptions must be made. Our case was special...both dogs knew each other well and other than Hilde's dominance over Blade, there should be no other issues. Yeah, right!

We had no intention of just letting the two dogs run loose together and mate on their own time schedule. We would control the breeding. Of course, neither Hilde nor Blade had any experience in this area and it wasn't possible to go out and rent a video for them. The fact that Hilde was dominant and would be calling the shots, presented the very real possibility of injury to either or both dogs. Wine, roses and soft music were not required and thus we decided to proceed step-by-step according to the book. It had not occurred to us that neither Blade nor Hilde had read the book!

We calculated the target date for the first breeding and Hilde was right on schedule. Good girl! Suddenly it appeared as if the breeding would be much easier than we had anticipated. I had three days off from work and that just happened to coincide with the optimum breeding dates, could things get any better? This was going to be a snap!

Soon Blade was performing his courtship dances and

we were impressed with his style. Boy did he strut his stuff! How could Hilde refuse such charm? Hilde was participating in her own version of the courtship dance, but always drew a line at a certain point. Blade would calm down for awhile and then repeat the performance. There were still two more days prior to the optimum breeding window according to the book. Back off, Blade, your time will come.

Finally the big day arrived and the two were brought together; Hilde said, "No!" Using the book as our guide, we tried the restraint method. That failed when Blade got too close to Hilde's teeth. The new muzzle was tried and that failed...Hilde was even WORSE while wearing the muzzle. She could not hurt him while wearing the muzzle, but her intimidation skills were unrestrained. After three days of failed efforts, I admitted defeat and tried to figure out how I could possibly have missed the dates. I returned to work with a heavy heart since it would be approximately six months before the next breeding attempt.

With the pressure off, we let the dogs resume their normal lives. Blade still persisted with his courtship routine and Hilde tolerated his frenzied actions, but no longer joined in with her version of the courtship dance. I dreaded the call to Sue and thus postponed it as long as possible. Oh well, maybe things will work out in August although we preferred a Spring breeding.

Two days later Bobbie called me at work to let me know that we no longer needed to worry about the dogs...they had achieved on their own what we had tried to control according to the book. The following day they repeated the performance for my benefit and life resumed its normal pace. Of course we were anxious to know if the breeding was successful. It would be roughly a month before Hilde would show signs of pregnancy. We babied her during this time and kept our fingers crossed. Hurry up and wait, again.

We thought we could see changes after a week had passed, but it was just wishful thinking. We even asked a pharmacist if one of the early pregnancy test kits would work and he was certain that it would, after all, it's really testing for the same thing. Hilde was not pleased that you-know-who was chasing her around the yard with the test strip each time she went out. And after all of that, it didn't work anyway. (No, I didn't get my money back.)

After thirty days had passed, we were certain that Hilde was pregnant; five days later there was no question! She grew steadily and we began to worry about restricting her activities. Sue said that Hilde would limit her activities automatically as she increased in size. Not our Hilde, she continued to impress us with her mobility until we took her to Camelot. She was never predictable; she was usually the exception to the rule.

As a rough approximation of her growth rate we looked at the gestation information and noted that gestation runs about sixty-three or sixty-four days. That equates to nine weeks or each week is the rough equivalent of one month for humans. That provided us with a rough approximation that we could readily use to anticipate her new feeding requirements. We needed only to increase the amount of food as she progressed. Supposedly she would be on double her normal ration as she neared her whelping date. We kept up her exercise routine until she really became obvious and then began to ease off. That really did not matter, she continued to run, jump and perform all manner of acrobatics as usual. Only in the final few days did she slow down and that was not by much.

We took her to the vet and he assured us that her weight was about normal and gave her a clean bill of health. He was unable to count the size of the litter and wanted to know if we were interested in an x-ray. We were concerned about any possible effects on the litter and he assured us that there was essentially no risk. We consented and watched as he counted seven and possibly eight pups. He informed us that they all appeared to be well-developed and very close in size. He saw no

problems. We breathed a huge sigh of relief.
Two days later we took Hilde to Camelot.

Chapter 15

The Puppies

The puppies were born April 22, 1999, four males and three females. Sue's phone call was truly a happy occasion...all were doing well and Hilde was settling into her role as an excellent new mother. We had worried about complications and there were none. There could not have been better news. While we were elated, we knew that it would be several weeks before we could visit Hilde and her pups. This was due to the possibility of our introducing something harmful into their area during a visit. Here was another instance of hurry up and wait, Hilde's trademark, again. We informed Blade of his new status, but he was not the least bit excited.

Finally, after what seemed like ages, Sue called and invited us over to meet the litter and visit with Hilde. The term "at your convenience" meant nothing to us; we did not care what time, day or night. We made the drive to Camelot in record time and Sue greeted us immediately upon our arrival so that Hilde would not become aware of our presence. Hilde and her offspring were doing well and Sue escorted us to a room adjacent to the special whelping rooms. There she explained that she would go in first and entice Hilde to leave the whelping box; then she would tell us to enter. This was to protect the puppies from Hilde's frenzied departure from the whelping box when she rushed to greet us. I perceived this added caution as being a little too extreme. Boy was I wrong! Sue later mentioned an incident where a puppy had been severely injured in just such a manner.

When Sue told us to come in, Hilde went absolutely crazy! She went to Bobbie and then to me. She ran and jumped.   There was no controlling her...she was so excited. She whined and cried! She jumped up on us and we loved it. Her heart and tail were both racing. It was both sad and heartwarming. It took a full twenty minutes for her to calm down. Sue left somewhere in the middle of the chaos and eventually everything returned to a casual, relaxed atmosphere. Hilde suddenly remembered the puppies and jumped into the whelping box. She sat and looked at us as if to say, "Look what I've got!"

Seven puppies were in the whelping box. Their eyes were open and they clumsily moved around attempting to nurse. The whelping box was approximately four feet by four feet with sides about ten inches high. Wooden dowels located approximately two and one-half inches from and parallel to the floor also extended the same distance from and parallel to each side of the box. This allowed the puppies to have some extra room if their mother accidentally laid down on them; they would not be crushed against the walls. Why would the mother lie down on her own puppies? Keeping tabs on the location of each puppy is difficult for the mother. Add movement to each puppy and the task becomes even more difficult. Finally, the possible consequences of misjudging the location of one or more puppies is not understood by the mother. A squeak or cry from a puppy would normally result in the mother moving while in the process of investigating and that could be enough to alleviate the problem.

Of course we had a camera with us and I immediately took a few quick snapshots. Bobbie sat down on the floor next to the whelping box and watched the puppies for a few minutes. It wasn't long before she reached over and picked up one of the pups. Hilde was looking in the opposite direction and I prepared for a photo of Bobbie holding the puppy with Hilde watching. Upon being picked up, the puppy squeaked and I just happened to be looking at Hilde through the viewfinder. I saw an extremely agitated Hilde turning her head toward Bobbie and I automatically clicked the shutter; I did not have enough time to shout a warning. As soon as Hilde realized that it was Bobbie holding the puppy, her anger subsided and she simply sniffed the puppy. Later, when the film was developed, we could still see some of the anger on Hilde's face although it had softened from what I had initially seen through the viewfinder. Bobbie and I both had assumed that we would automatically be allowed to handle the puppies without incident. This was our first indication that Hilde had changed as a result of motherhood.

We watched her tend to her offspring and marveled at her tenderness and competence. Once she had taken care of the needs of her puppies, she returned to visit with us. Any noise from the puppies brought an instantaneous reaction from Hilde. The pups always took priority over us.

We marveled at the puppies. They were solid and either constantly moving or sound asleep. Hilde would survey the whelping box and then gingerly jump right in. After a quick survey of the area, she would quickly flop down on her side so that the puppies could nurse. Immediately seven small puppies would descend upon her and begin nursing. They constantly maneuvered for a better position and when full would move into two groups piling up on top of each other and falling asleep. Hilde would clean the puppies while they nursed and double-check each one as they slept. It was humbling to witness her maternal instincts and her concern for the welfare of her brood. We were overwhelmed by our "perfect puppy." This was my first real observation of a canine litter and it was simply incredible, probably because it included a member of our household.

Leaving was extremely difficult. We postponed our departure as long as possible, but finally realized that it would be better to leave. It actually became awkward, similar to those times when you visit someone and everyone runs out of things to say. We were not able to play with the puppies...they were just too young. Perhaps we knew how difficult the departure would be and we did have a two-hour drive awaiting us. As we prepared for our departure, Hilde assumed that we were taking her home and whined and barked when we left her room. She came out into her outside pen and cried as we walked to the Blazer. It was truly a heartbreaking experience. She was still looking when we drove out of sight.

The puppies grew and eventually it was time for them to leave for their new homes. We had purposely avoided the kennel because of the difficulty in leaving Hilde. We desperately wanted to see the puppies, but we knew that it was better to stay away. Finally, Sue called and said that we could come get Hilde. Luckily, we were able to see the last of the puppies prior to its leaving for its new home. She was cute as all puppies are and seemed to have a good disposition. We played with her for awhile and then loaded an extremely happy Hilde for the trip back home. She constantly pawed the divider that restricted her to the back of the Blazer and stayed as close to us as possible. She did not take a nap on the trip home. She knew where she was headed.

We wondered about the puppies. Did they go to good homes? Did they resemble Blade or were they more like Hilde? Sue provided a list of the puppies' owners and we were able to contact all but one family. We agreed to exchange photos and provided the new owners with photos of Hilde and Blade along with a summary of the two dogs. We still maintain contact with several of the families. It was a good experience, but we were glad that it was over. Hilde was home.

Chapter 16

Lulu – The Little Tornado

As Hilde's whelping date had grown closer, we realized that Blade would need a playmate. As long as we were able to remain within his view, he was fine; that was not always possible. We have always had little tolerance for barking dogs...especially nuisance barking. Consequently, we did not want complaints from the neighbors when Blade barked and Blade was guaranteed to bark! With both of us working, a large percentage of the day would require Blade to be outside. We were reluctant to leave him in the house alone since a bored Weimie can invent some spectacular self-entertainment! Blade had never resorted to destructive binges, but there was the very real possibility that an extended absence of his human family could result in some serious damage to the house or furnishings. Leaving him outside could also result in his departure as he had demonstrated several times! Another solution was to take Blade wherever we went and this was not always practical. Of course, we could also stay home, but that wasn't practical, either. We discussed this problem with Sue and she mentioned that a temporary female puppy would be the best solution. This would be a win-win-win solution: Blade would have a playmate, we would retain our sanity and the puppy would gain a new experience.

Blade probably would not tolerate another male while any female should be acceptable. If the female were clearly younger, Blade could be dominant over another dog for the first time in his life. It just so happened that Sue had two young females who were Hilde's half-sisters, a fact that might accelerate the acceptance factor. She referred to them as "Thelma and Louise." My immediate mental picture was two Weimaraners in a convertible driving over the edge of a cliff. Sue quickly explained that the two were inseparable and one was called Lulu. It was worth a try. Lulu was the designated trial dog.

A few days before her due date we headed for Camelot with a very large Hilde and a very unsuspecting Blade. We took a crate, just in case Blade and his new companion did not become immediate friends. We coined a new phrase for this Hilde-substitute: rent-a-dog.

Both dogs calmly endured the ride although we thought that we detected a little uneasiness in Hilde. Approaching Camelot, both dogs realized where they were and became extremely excited. Both were soon to undergo major changes in their lives. We said our good-byes to Hilde who was reluctant to let us go...not that she had much say in the matter. We then let Blade become acquainted with Lulu in a large pen. After they finished their sniffing routine and calmed down somewhat, we put Lulu in the crate and let Blade have the remainder of the Blazer. Lulu was so happy with her new playmate! Blade, however, seemed confused about this intruder and showed mild indifference punctuated with occasional moments of extreme curiosity. At some point in time, Blade marked the crate...something that we did not find especially endearing. The drive home was otherwise uneventful (Well, we did buy a boat). There was no barking or growling...at least not between the dogs.

Lulu adjusted to her temporary home very quickly. She investigated the layout of the house and yard and settled into her own routine. She was an affectionate puppy with boundless energy and she had no bad habits. She had two "accidents" before she learned to signal her need to go outdoors and then she was fine. Apparently she missed her sister and sought canine companionship from the only other available source: Blade. He just tried to avoid Lulu, but she would approach him clearly displaying a desire to play. Blade initially ignored her and she would press the issue until he emitted a low growl. She would then back off for a few minutes. He just would not play with her. She tried constantly to change his mind and this continued for two days. On the third day she changed her tactic: she crouched in the "let's play" posture, hesitated for a few seconds and then charged right at Blade! It happened so quickly that I could not intervene; I braced myself for the carnage which was certain to occur. Severe injury or death was probable...she was no match for his size and power! How would we explain it to Sue?

Lulu never touched Blade...he raced away with the "little tornado" in hot pursuit! Around, over and on the furniture, always slightly ahead, Blade obviously prided himself in his speed and strength! Lulu on the other hand was far more agile and eventually caught him. Blade then became the pursuer and the game began anew. Bobbie and I alternated between laughing and yelling for the two to slow down. Eventually we persuaded them to go outside and the game reached new heights. Both dogs collapsed after several intensive minutes and took a quick nap. The "little tornado" awoke first and immediately went after Blade. Almost twice her weight, Blade just needed more recuperation time. He reluctantly resumed the game and soon was thoroughly enjoying the fun once again. Both dogs slept well that night! The next day was a continuation of the previous day. The change in Blade was mind-boggling...the "couch potato" was changed forever. She ran him to exhaustion and he loved every minute of it. There was no need for him to constantly seek our attention and he usually ignored us altogether unless summoned. He still required some human contact, but Lulu was clearly his preference.

We tried our best to figure out what had triggered this sudden change in attitude in Blade until we realized that Hilde had never really played with Blade. Perhaps it was beneath her dignity to play with someone junior to her in the pack. Maybe she simply did not know how to play with another dog. Once Blade was forced into playing chase, he began to enjoy those puppy games that he had missed. Every day Lulu would add some new aspect to their play. The down side was that Blade weighed more than seventy pounds and that is a really BIG puppy. Put him in the house and playing hard and you have a very scary but very funny situation. Having learned to jump over the loveseat or to use it as a springboard to the sofa, Blade never checked first to see if either was occupied prior to commencing a romp. Trust me when I say that the sight of Blade sailing through the air inches from your face was a real attention-getter! Above all, we learned not to move if we were seated on the sofa or loveseat and heard him coming! Lulu was no threat; she was forced to run around most of the furniture.

Lulu stole "his" toys, ambushed him and barked at him if he tried to ignore her. She made a short career of converting this shy, well-mannered adult into a crazy yet adorable overgrown puppy. At the same time he provided safety and reassurance when she was frightened by some new and/or scary situation.

During our various outings, she was exposed to dozens of new places and experiences and would usually mimic most of Blade's actions. Lulu was in her glory when on a leash. She captivated people everywhere and relished the extra attention. She was just a happy dog meeting lots of new people. Occasionally she would act shy around some individuals, but usually she would pull against the leash to lavish affection on these new friends that she was about to meet. One of her favorite excursions was to the vintage car displays at the local Wal-Mart on Monday evenings. She was fearless when some of the louder cars arrived and motorcycles were a major curiosity. Blade, on the other hand, did not care for the motorcycles, but tolerated the cars and hotrods without any problems. He was always as close to Lulu as he could get, possibly to allay her fears or maybe to reduce his own. Being male and an "unknown quantity," Blade was viewed which great suspicion by the owners of the vehicles! If he even LOOKED at the wheels, we were asked to please keep him away from the cars. Thus we received a LOT of verbal and non-verbal communication concerning that potential problem although it was invariably in good fun. Blade had been taught not to mark while on a leash except when given permission, a fact, which was unknown to the vehicle owners. Lulu, on the other hand, was not considered a threat and was welcome anywhere and by everyone.

Blade began to assume his role as the dominant dog mostly from a protective point of view. I never saw him discipline her, but she seemed to sense where the line was and that it would be unwise to cross it. Blade did not allow Lulu to touch him when he slept and so she would pick the nearest human available and lean against them until she fell asleep. She seemed to need the touch of another animal and if Blade wouldn't allow it, she would seek attention elsewhere. Of course, we ate it up. It was really hard to adjust to that side of Lulu. She probably missed her sister. Like Hilde, she was very expressive with her face and knew how to turn on the charm. Moments of aggravation because of some of her actions were quickly replaced by smiles as she put on her best remorseful face...she knew exactly what she was doing! We didn't care. We fell in love with the "little tornado" which was something we had not anticipated. She became far more than just a temporary replacement for Hilde.

As luck would have it, Sue needed Lulu back at the kennel for some pre-show training. Hilde was still caring for her litter and Blade still needed a companion. We drove Lulu to Camelot to exchange her for another female. As a parting shot, Lulu left her mark (literally) on a cushion in the Blazer...the only aggravation she ever caused us. The "little tornado" later moved to California and subsequently entered the show ring where she did well. We owe her a great debt. Blade gained confidence and tolerance while having an extraordinary good time. Thank you, Lulu.

Luckily Sue had a substitute named Gabby who easily adapted to Blade, our house and to us. She was a beautiful female, taller than Blade and just quiet, comfortable and lovable. This new "rent-a-dog" was strikingly elegant and so very different from Lulu. Blade treated her as an equal almost immediately and probably enjoyed the slower pace. We relished the relative quiet for a few days, but began to miss the complete chaos that Lulu brought.

Chapter 17

Hilde Comes Home and Leaves

Hilde was happy to return home and both dogs seemed glad to be back in their old routines. That is not completely true...Blade had learned to enjoy his role as "top dog" and apparently assumed that he would remain in that position. Hilde, on the other hand, was unaware that she had relinquished any claim to the throne and thus the stage was set for the inevitable confrontation. When it arrived, it was over almost immediately with Hilde the undisputed "top dog" and Blade no longer forced to worry about maintaining his title! This brings up the question asked by anyone who has ever owned a show dog: why does my dog only get injured or bitten on the side that the judge sees? Perhaps it is a huge coincidence, but Blade has NEVER received any injury to his right side...only the left side.

With our help, Hilde began a serious attempt to regain her girlish figure, but gravity and nature had changed her forever. At Bobbie's urging, there will no further discussion of that topic!

Bobbie's sister and her family dropped by one evening for a visit as they had done on many occasions. They were cautioned that Hilde had experienced a change in attitude since the birth of her puppies. I recommended that they not crowd her if she indicated that she wanted to be alone. My nephew, Paul, received the first surprise. He wore a strange hat into the house and Hilde came unglued! We were finally able to calm her down by removing the hat. Later, she growled at Carl when he elected to sit too close to her. Even Bobbie's sister, Paula, received a warning snap when she crowded Hilde a little too much. Paula stated that Hilde had tried to bite her; I assured her that Hilde doesn't miss and it was simply a warning.

The grand finale again involved Paul. He put the hat back on and got right in Hilde's face to say good bye to her. Unfortunately, she was asleep and awoke just as he approached her face. He received a nip to the chin as a reminder not to do that! I was amazed that he would do such a thing after being warned and knowing Hilde's reaction to his mom's crowding episode. If he had not been moving toward Hilde's face or if she had room to maneuver, he would not have received the nip. Yes, Hilde had definitely changed.

* *

At a recent major dog show, Sue mentioned to us that she had met an individual with whom she had discussed Field Trials and Hilde's name had come up due to her background. She asked if we were interested in sending Hilde to Ohio for Field Trial training. Dan and Cindy Long had excellent reputations in the area of training and specialized in training Weimaraners. Hilde was constantly demonstrating her desire to hunt, but we were not too enthusiastic about sending her away again since she had just returned home. We reluctantly agreed, however, telling ourselves that her genes and instincts were somehow demanding that she be allowed to do what she was bred to do. Hey, it sounded good...at least in theory. We resigned ourselves to another long separation.

Hilde's training date grew closer and suddenly it was time to leave for Ohio. Another individual was sending his female Weimaraner and we agreed to take her with us since we had plenty of room. At the last minute Sue informed us that the other dog was also an "alpha" and a cover for the crate was needed to keep the two from seeing each other. Well that got our attention! The Blazer was certainly large enough, but not if a barking and growling contest was virtually guaranteed for the entire thirteen-hour trip. Secretly we knew that the situation could not really be that bad since there is always that tendency to overstate a bad situation so that you feel better about the whole mess when it's all over. Boy, were we wrong!

We arrived at Camelot early on that summer day with Blade and Hilde. Blade would be remaining at the kennel and we would pick him up on the way home. After watching Blade go to his kennel we were introduced to Keta. She seemed sweet and docile and we loaded her into the crate while Hilde made her potty run. We knew that Hilde was a good traveler, but Keta was an unknown. We did not know if she was skilled in indicating her need to stop and so we made plans to stop approximately every two hours to allow the dogs to stretch and relieve themselves as necessary. As soon as Hilde re-entered the Blazer, "Keta the Hun" conveyed to her that she was capable of and would relish the opportunity to remove Hilde from the face of the earth! Bobbie and I both clearly understood that message even though most people would have heard only a dog growling. It wasn't so much WHAT Keta said, but HOW she said it. My blood ran cold even though the morning was warm.

With Hilde outside the Blazer once again, I put the drape over the crate so that the two would not be able to view each other. Keta was her charming self again and Hilde re-entered the Blazer. "Keta the Hun" quietly reminded Hilde of her ultimate goal followed by complete silence. This was the proverbial "calm before the storm." Soon we were on the road.

It was quiet for the first two hours and we began to relax. It appeared that the two dogs had reached some sort of understanding. Suddenly "Keta the Hun" exploded into action and Hilde responded although somewhat quieter. Automatically, I told Hilde (actually both dogs) to be quiet and Hilde immediately silenced; either "quiet" or "no" was all that was required for her. Unfortunately, "Keta the Hun" either did not understand me or chose not to obey me. I went through a series of commands that I thought she might obey, but none worked. The noise made the Blazer seem so much smaller than it actually was and we were becoming fearful of being crushed as the vehicle appeared to shrink as the volume increased. In spite of what I had been taught as a young boy, I shouted something which I had been forbidden to say: "Shut up!"

"Keta the Hun" immediately reverted to sweet and gentle Keta. The silence was frightening...I thought that I had killed her! Oh, no...what do we do now? Wow! "Shut up" worked and was not required again.

Armed with our newly acquired noise solution, we continued our journey almost without incident. We did learn that during the canine potty stops that both dogs were to be kept apart and that Hilde was now convinced that she could ruin Keta's day if given the opportunity.

When we finally reached our destination, we made it clear that those two must be kept apart. This was ultimately honored except on two later occasions with each dog winning once. While we discussed the training process and other items, we communicated Hilde's love of any game involving tennis balls as a method of gaining her trust. Hilde had demonstrated a complete refusal to listen and respond to anyone except members of her pack. This would be a major hindrance to the training effort until she accepted Dan and Cindy. That would take the better part of a month.

Once again we prepared for the departure ritual with Hilde and it was not any easier than before. Even though she could not see us from the kennel, she knew we were there. After an extensive discussion on her training, financial requirements and keeping us up to date on Hilde's progress, we left. Hilde heard the Blazer engine start and knew that something was happening, but without her. Here she was in a strange environment and her family was leaving. We heard her cries and sadly departed, telling ourselves how much she would enjoy her training. We located a place to spend the night and quickly fell asleep from exhaustion, both physical and mental.

The trip home was long, but much quieter.

Chapter 18

Star - Quite the Attraction

It was time for another rent-a-dog. Once again Sue came to the rescue only this time it was with Lulu's sister...the other half of "Thelma and Louise." The association between "Lulu" and "Louise" had been readily apparent; however, we could not figure out any name that would associate with Thelma EXCEPT Thelma! I decided that I would never call her name if she were outdoors. I do have my pride.

The drive back from Ohio had been relatively easy and it was only slightly out of our way to stop by Camelot and pick up Blade and THELMA. Of course Blade was thrilled to be going home and was not aware that he would be traveling with the new rent-a-dog. We put him in an outdoor pen and Sue's son, Eric, brought out Blade's new friend and called her "Star." I informed him that THELMA was supposedly going with us and he said, "No, her name is Star...Camelot's Star Attraction."

I was certainly relieved and Blade was clearly pleased with his new housemate. They were best of friends in only minutes. Perhaps it was Lulu's influence or maybe it was just that Blade was happy to have a new playmate. Of course there was the possibility that he was glad it was Star and not Hilde and her sharp teeth! We put Star in the crate for the trip home since there was the possibility that the two would not get along well. It was not necessary, Star wagged her tail constantly and pawed at Blade through the crate...it was truly a sight to behold. This was going to be a good experience for all of us.

After an uneventful drive, Star entered our house and walked through every room with Blade accompanying her. She completed her inspection and proceeded to the backdoor and looked at me. I clearly understood her silent request although I was surprised that she knew where the exit point was. Once outside, she took care of business and explored the entire yard. This was going to be another incredible experience...a dog with good manners. As soon as she had first entered the house, she was completely at ease and never suffered any anxiety. We had never encountered such complete, immediate trust by an animal; it was almost as if she had always been a member of our household.

We left both dogs outside for awhile and Star continued her exploration. Blade accompanied her, but was not constantly bothering her as he had done with Lulu and Gabby. They played for awhile and we relaxed our vigilance since there was no apparent need for concern. Eventually, Blade barked to come inside and was followed by our newest guest. Star conducted another survey of the house and picked up a toy which she brought into the living room and commenced to chew. Blade calmly climbed up on the sofa having decided to take a nap and Star decided to do the same. For some reason she chose not to jump up on the sofa, but looked at Blade and then at me. It was obvious that she wanted to curl up on the sofa. I told her "Okay," expecting her to hop right up beside Blade. Either she did not understand or did not trust me. We had not asked Sue about her policy regarding dogs on the furniture. I finally picked up Star and placed her on the sofa. She watched me warily for a few minutes, adjusted her position and dozed off.

I previously mentioned that Blade did not allow another dog to touch him when he slept. This was true even with Lulu in spite of his fondness for her. So it was quite a surprise a few minutes later to see that Star had moved and was sound asleep with her head resting on Blade's hip. I walked over to move her, trying not to awaken Blade in the process. I was startled and a little anxious when Blade raised his head, looked at me, looked at Star and lowered his head, resuming his nap. Even

Bobbie was surprised. Perhaps Blade was ill. Ultimately, Star was allowed to rest her head on Blade and that remained true on all three occasions that she visited with us.

There was absolutely no conflict between the two dogs. There was not even any jealousy over Blade's toys which were actually Hilde's toys when she was home! Both dogs ate their meals with essentially no supervision even though Blade could have easily taken Star's food. Later, Sue mentioned that Star must be fed in her crate, but we had been watching them and saw no need; we never had a problem.

Star was not as rambunctious as Lulu had been. She seemed to instinctively know Blade's favorite game and soon she was chasing him and vice versa. They played hard, but Star was much more gentle and seemed to know when to stop and rest...something that Lulu had never demonstrated. It became obvious that Blade preferred her company to that of his human "pack" and thus always remained near Star. She, on the other hand, was always eager to please her new family members and quickly won our hearts. What a charmer! She had not yet reached her adult size, but her sleek, elegant lines were very impressive and it was obvious that she would soon be in the show ring and winning.

The responsibility of transporting and caring for a breeder's dog was something that had a very sobering effect on us. We were constantly on the lookout for anything that could jeopardize the safety of our own dogs, but the safety of a dog belonging to Sue always weighed heavily on our minds. Although we realized that accidents could and do happen, there would always be tough questions to answer. Luckily there was never an accident or injury of any sort.

A few days after Star's arrival, I returned from work and noticed some assorted dog toys and a beef hoof or two in a small pile on the living room floor. I assumed that Bobbie had gathered them for relocation to a basket or other container and had been interrupted. To my surprise she mentioned that the pile had just appeared. The next day I noticed a similar pile of various items in the backyard. While I stood there, Star walked to the pile and added a pinecone. Star was a collector and required some sort of order in her life! This was something unique to Star and she repeated this behavior on a regular basis. This was the first time that we had encountered a dog who considered neatness to be a virtue.

Star had no bad habits. She was just absolutely perfect and never created any type of problem. She used less facial expression than Lulu or Hilde, but her tail constantly wagged and she absolutely LOVED to hear her name. She looked forward to rides and was an excellent traveler. Whereas Lulu LIKED the vintage car excursions to Wal-Mart, Star LOVED them. She enjoyed meeting people and always tried to drag us to the next group. Invariably we would be asked her name and it would be repeated; that was her cue to rush to these new humans and display an immediate joy and affection that was simply incredible. She just drew crowds with her loving antics. No one seemed to mind the fact that she jumped on them because of her genuinely joyful greeting. At first we had tried to prevent her from jumping up on people, but we were told that it was "okay" so many times that we gave up. We are certain that some individuals did not want her to jump up on them, but they apparently just stayed out of the way or gave in to her charm.

During this same time Blade was patiently greeting people , but not with that same enthusiasm. Perhaps he was just waiting for that dreaded motorcycle that he knew was going to be started nearby and he just could not seem to be convinced that motorcycles were okay. The owners of the various vintage vehicles welcomed Star, but upon seeing Blade and noticing that he was a male, "requested" once again that we keep him away from their wheels! We endured more good-natured kidding in that respect. Some things never change.

Star did provide us with two surprises. On one occasion as I entered her field of vision, she gave me a long, extended bark. This was not a series of single barks, this was something unique. Prior to that she had only barked on rare occasions and usually because Blade initiated the barking. This was something totally different and Bobbie and I laughed. Her tail wagged ferociously while doing this. We encouraged it simply because it was so funny and she seemed to enjoy it also. The second surprise was not so funny.

Hilde's favorite toy from her early puppy days had been a yellow rubber duck which we called "Ducky" just to distinguish it from the other toys that she would fetch by name. The duck was obviously chew-proof since Hilde still had it after two years and Blade was not allowed to even LOOK at it, much less touch it. Star destroyed the duck in one attempt during her first week. Only the head and front part of the body could be located...the rest just disappeared. This was clearly a message to someone...perhaps to Hilde. That was the extent of Star's destructive habits, at least from our point of view. Okay, so she wasn't exactly perfect.

Chapter 19

The First Hunt Test

After the Field Trial training, several people advised me to get Hilde started in Hunt Tests, but I had no idea what a Hunt Test was. Of course, a few years ago I didn't know what a show ring was either. Hilde had not returned with instructions or an operating manual, leaving me with a very small knowledge base to work from. I had never been exposed to hunting with a trained dog and thus had no experience to draw upon. The original plan had been for us to drive to Ohio, receive some "hands on" training and return with Hilde. Instead, a unique set of events brought her to Camelot where we happily picked her up without benefit of any instruction. Regardless, we were elated to have her home.

Several days after her return from Ohio, I took her to a large field to see how she responded to commands. I was reluctant to remove the leash since she had learned months ago that I could not enforce the "come" command when she was loose. Armed with my very limited hunting vocabulary, I finally took a deep breath, unsnapped the leash and told her to "Go hunt!" Hilde took off and immediately went into a hunting mode. Okay, that seemed to work. Things were looking good. I used the "Whoa" command and she instantly froze in a point with her right front paw raised. I then said, "Okay," which had been her release from her stacked pose in the ring and she resumed hunting. I tried directing her left and right with hand signals and she responded immediately.

Gaining confidence in her responses, I began walking and she immediately established her pattern based on my movement. Wow, I was impressed! I made announced and unannounced turns and she responded quickly and what appeared to be appropriately. This was far beyond my wildest hopes! Finally, it was time for the moment of truth...would she come when called? "Hilde, come!" She was at my side in seconds and awaiting her next command. I cannot explain the relief I felt. I was grinning so hard that my face hurt. This was one dog who had always allowed herself to be collared only after she had explored anything and everything that she desired. To say that I was overjoyed would have been a gross understatement.

We resumed "hunting" and worked our way back toward the Blazer. I gave her some water and left her loose just to see what she would do. She stayed nearby so I opened the tailgate and said "Load up." She did. I rushed home, grabbed Bobbie and drove to a small open area not too far from our home. I didn't even bother with the leash; I opened the tailgate and told Hilde to "Go hunt" and off she went.

Bobbie was extremely nervous since we had parked on the side of a moderately traveled road. It was never an issue...Hilde was completely changed and responded just as she had minutes earlier. I demonstrated everything we had previously done and called her back several times. Bobbie was impressed. We returned home happy and smug with our "new" Hilde. Now it was time to put this new knowledge to work.

I located and read material on AKC hunt tests and downloaded the hunt test rules from the Internet. Bobbie and I then found a scheduled Hunt Test in Connecticut and since it wasn't too far away, decided to give up part of a weekend to check it out. There we ran into Sue O'Donnell who had handled both Hilde and Blade in the show ring while helping Sue Thomas. She and her husband trained hunting dogs in addition to showing some in the ring. Sue explained basically how the hunt tests were conducted and pointed out a better location to observe the tests.

Trying to observe the hunt tests from a distance was

not too enlightening and at her urging, I walked the course with her as part of the gallery. I was prepared to ask her if she or her husband would consider handling Hilde in a hunt test after providing her with some additional training. I waited for a better opportunity to bring up the subject.

By the time we finished observing the two dogs and their handlers, I realized that I could act as Hilde's handler and decided to enter the next available Junior Hunt Test. The process did not look difficult and Hilde supposedly knew what she was doing; that was enough for me. I reasoned that the worst thing I could do would be to embarrass myself and, heck, I've done that before. Actually, I have a LOT of experience in that area!

AKC hunt tests are divided into three levels: Junior which is entry level with four graded areas, Senior which is more advanced with six graded areas and finally Master which is the most precise and most difficult with the same six graded areas as Senior. Each successive level requires more from the dog while reducing direction or assistance from the handler. Dogs are judged against a standard, not each other. Two dogs, two handlers and two judges constitute a "brace" and numerous braces are run during hunt tests. In the Junior Hunt Test both dogs are turned loose and the handlers work them around to the bird field where pen-raised quail are "planted" by another individual. The two judges follow and observe the dogs. The dog must find and "point" a quail and the handler must inform the judge that the dog is pointing. The dog must then remain steady while the handler draws a blank pistol and "flushes" the quail. The handler then fires the blank pistol. That checks to see if the dog is "gun shy" or afraid of the sound. Obviously this would not be a desirable trait in a hunting dog! The four graded areas are Hunting, Bird Finding Ability, Pointing and Trainability. There is also a time limit. This is a very brief explanation. If you are a glutton for punishment, look it up on the Web!

I began working with Hilde in the local stocked game

fields even though stocking had not yet begun for the season. Surely there would be a few residual or native quail there. We spent several sessions hoping to encounter at least one bird. Either there were no quail there or Hilde just couldn't locate them. Look, Hilde, this is a PICTURE of a quail; that didn't seem to help. Maybe a BETTER picture....

I bought a training dummy and a bottle of quail scent from a local sporting goods store and took Hilde to a large open area where we warmed up with some basic hand and voice commands. I then "planted" the scented training dummy and worked Hilde around to where she could pick up the scent. She quickly located the dummy and pointed it. I approached her, told her to stay, grabbed the training dummy and slung it as far as possible. Just as it commenced a downward trajectory I yelled "bang" and waited for it to hit the ground. Then I told her to "Go fetch!" She took off, located the dummy and brought it back, carefully placing it in my outstretched hand. We did this several times until I knew that she could find and retrieve a scented dummy. Her hunting patterns looked good and she followed voice and hand signals well so I bought the requisite starter's pistol. A .22 caliber? Heck no, a .380 makes **more noise!**

The day of that first hunt test soon arrived and while I was somewhat nervous, Hilde was calm but perhaps a little excited about the presence of the other dogs. Hilde's bracemate was a very shy Irish Setter bitch who was informed by Hilde with a stare that she was an "alpha." What would happen when the two dogs were released? Would Hilde go after the Irish Setter? Suddenly I was really nervous. Visions of everything that could possibly go wrong flooded my mind. "Relax, just let Hilde do her thing." Bobbie's words were appreciated, but had absolutely no calming effect on me. Advice from other handlers was very simple: "Don't over-control her...let her training and instincts drive her." Well then, why does she need a handler? What if I mess things up for her?

After what seemed an eternity, our two judges called for our brace and we joined them with a mixture of excitement and dread (Hilde had the excitement; I had the dread). The other handler was perfectly calm and seemed to be bored by the whole process. The judges discussed the course and asked if there were questions. I informed the judges that this was my first hunt test and one stated that they would be judging Hilde...not me. I took that as some leeway should I commit some error short of total disqualification.

We moved down the road in a group. Then came the moment of truth: we were told to turn the dogs loose. I crossed my fingers mentally and released Hilde. There was no cause for concern, she was there to hunt and apparently the other dog was not of any interest. Off they went with Hilde on the left and the Irish Setter on the right. Everything was going well and I began to relax.

If Hilde ranged too far on the setter's side I would move her back. This was not a requirement, just a courtesy. On one of those wide swings I called Hilde's name just as she stopped. She turned and glared at me just as I motioned her to move to the left. Something was wrong! I repeated the signal. Instead of her normal instantaneous turn and quick response, she looked ahead and then moved forward, making a wide, sweeping turn back toward me. Surprise! She flushed a quail in the process, which she COMPLETELY IGNORED. A little voice inside me said, "Uh oh." I glanced toward both judges who were staring at me in utter disbelief. "I might have been a little premature," I said sheepishly and watched them nod their heads. Gotta give her a little more discretion...let her do her own thing.

Moments later I again moved Hilde from right to left and at a pile of logs and debris directly in front of me, she chose to go OVER rather than around. At mid-point in the jump she turned her head and looked at me. There was that look, a combination of aggravation and/or disgust that most Weimaraner owners have seen as their dog passed judgment on them. She then turned her head

129

back to complete the jump. I glanced at the judge nearest to me and noted a huge grin...the judge had seen it too. I would have given Hilde a "10" for the jump, but deducted 2 for giving me "the look."

Several minutes later we entered the bird field and shortly thereafter Hilde slowed her movement and eased into a very sad point with her right hind leg raised. She then turned and looked at me. Oh no, not "the look" again. I was certain the judge knew that Hilde was not pointing a bird...at least not with any confidence. On the other hand, I did not want to move her if there was even a remote possibility that a quail was actually there. I don't know why, maybe it was because of "the look," but I said to Hilde, "Don't look at me, you're the one with the great nose." She immediately resumed hunting and I once again glanced at the judge who said with a grin, "You actually TALK to your dog, don't you?" I could feel my ears turning red! "Yes."

Seconds later while moving away on my left, Hilde violently reversed direction, moved approximately ten feet and whirled back to the left and slammed into the kind of point you only see in hunting magazines. Wow and hallelujah! I called the point (even though I felt foolish doing so), drew the blank pistol and eased up to flush the quail.

I saw the quail just out of Hilde's view and staring straight at me. I moved to the side and then toward the quail hoping that he wouldn't run down the game trail where he was standing. Instead, he dropped into a small depression in the ground followed by TWO others. Life was good! I stepped into the depression, the three birds flushed, I paused for a second and squeezed the trigger. **The stupid pistol wouldn't fire!** Panic! Am I allowed to yell "bang?" I pulled the pistol down. What, the stupid trigger AND hammer frozen?? I feverishly worked the cylinder, finally heard it "click," raised the pistol even with my right ear and fired. Oh yeah, MUCH louder than a .22! The ringing stopped a few minutes later. The headache took a lot longer to subside.

I glanced over at Hilde who had been following the flight of the birds...they were landing just as I fired the pistol. She turned toward me and there was "the look" again. I made a mental note to apologize to Hilde later...when the judge couldn't hear it; I think the judge was getting nervous by this time. I told Hilde to "Go hunt" and off she went. Almost immediately the judge told me to pick up my dog. This was my cue to leave the bird field while she compared notes with the other judge. I was certain that Hilde had qualified...at least she had completed the four requirements. There was not the slightest hint from the judge.

It suddenly dawned on me that I had not seen the Irish Setter or the other handler since entering the bird field. Apparently I had been oblivious to everything else. I then realized that the other handler was calling his dog who had decided to hunt somewhere other than the bird field. Eventually, she returned and we left the bird field together. I told the other handler that I was certain that Hilde had qualified, even though the judge had not actually stated that as fact. The Irish Setter had not qualified since she had not located a single quail and had stopped following her handler's commands. Her handler was not the least bit upset leading me to believe that her entry was just a gamble.

The bird field bordered on the parking lot which meant that most spectators had an excellent view of the most critical part of the hunt test. Bobbie asked me why I had waited so long to fire the pistol and I told her about the problem. The same question came up several times; spectators at hunt tests are far more critical than spectators at dog shows! Bobbie also wanted to know if Hilde had qualified...and I was not certain

The two judges had finished comparing notes and assigning scores so Hilde and I worked our way over to the tent where the status board was located. We watched as they placed a "Q" in the block next to Hilde's name. Piece of cake...when's the next hunt test? This was fun! Moments later they presented us with the ribbon signifying a qualifying score. I was elated, but Hilde could not have cared less, so we went home.

Chapter 20

Hunting With Hilde

With one successful Hunt Test under my belt and with Hilde fully aware of what was expected, we entered two more Hunt Tests. Was I a little cocky? Hey, just go out and do the same thing as before. After all, it was not rocket science or brain surgery. I had absolutely no concern about subsequent Hunt Tests after seeing Hilde in action.

My friend, Mark, wanted to go quail hunting on Thanksgiving morning. We had hunted one afternoon early in the quail season and Hilde had picked up the scent of one quail that ran down a game trail and refused to flush. Eventually the quail flew into an area full of trees and Hilde was unable to reacquire the scent. This hunt would be a chance for her to redeem herself. It would also be good practice for Hilde right before the next Hunt Tests! And best of all, we would be hunting at the site of the previous hunt test. There should be ample quail around. There would also be some pheasant from that stocking program. This would be an opportunity to see Hilde in a more realistic setting as opposed to the artificial constraints of the Hunt Tests. At least that is what I envisioned. Above all, I wanted Mark to see Hilde in action.

Thanksgiving dawned with overcast skies and a light mist. The drive to the hunting area was filled with eager anticipation and Hilde was certainly excited. Mark and I discussed our simple game plan to ensure that we were both confident in what we were about to do. Mark also works at the power plant and carries several different weapons on a daily basis so I was not worried about his gun handling skills from a safety point of view. He is also a successful hunter.

I was certain that very few hunters would show up due to the weather and my assumption that few people were aware of this special hunting area. Unfortunately, **half of the population of the state was also there to hunt.** And EVERYBODY brought at least one dog! And **everybody brought a shotgun**; well, I didn't bring one...I brought Blade and a long lead to give him some hunting exposure. Perhaps Blade would suddenly show some hunting aspirations. It was worth a try.

Dog talent ranged from seasoned hunting dogs to family pets out for some exercise; human talent was an UNKNOWN and **everybody had a gun.** Milling around in the parking lot, some of the other hunters were a little careless with where their shotguns were pointed and we could only hope that they were not loaded...the shotguns, that is; of course we hoped that the hunters weren't loaded either.

Although the signs posted by the wildlife management office advised of the requirement to wait until official sunrise before departing the parking lot, most hunters and dogs left early (If you can't SEE the sunrise, apparently you can go early). " Hey Mark, tell those guys it's still twenty minutes before sunrise." "You do it!"

First shots were fired fifteen minutes prior to sunrise (and remember, **everybody had a gun.**) We finally left the parking lot and headed for a gap in the sea of orange vests and caps (**and guns**). We had the only dog controlled by voice commands and the sheer number of whistle blasts was creating some interesting dog movements!

We watched an overly eager dog flush a quail which flew past several hunters who were completely unaware of its approach...luckily no one saw it and took a shot (**even though everybody had a gun.**)! Most of the birds had moved to the edge of the tree lines and brush areas and these locations were receiving heavy attention from the hunters. The quail were more apt to be STEPPED ON than shot! Some of the tree lines were only about thirty feet wide and it was more than a little disconcerting to see other hunters coming from the opposite direction (**because they all had guns**). I felt somewhat naked being the only unarmed person in the area.

On one of these occasions a friendly black Labrador Retriever chose to come visit us because he really wasn't hunting anyway. Since he was coming rather fast, I recalled Hilde hoping that she wouldn't consider his rapid approach as an attack. Blade was still on the long lead but I had pulled him in when I first saw the Lab. I shouted to the approaching hunter to recall his dog just in case (**even though he had a gun**). He chose not to do so. Blade moved to a position directly between me and the approaching Lab, hair standing on end with head lowered while Hilde moved a little closer. I quickly said, "Hilde, stay" and "Blade, no" with a sharp jerk of the long lead. The Lab ignored Blade's defensive posture until the very last second...too late! He tried to reverse direction and slid to a stop at Blade's feet. Blade reached down and gave him a solid nip that sent the Lab racing back to his master (**he knew he had a gun!**). Blade made no attempt to pursue...he had protected his master and wagged his tail when I told him, "Good boy" (in a QUIET voice **because of the gun**). I told Hilde to "Go hunt" and she resumed her task. We worked our way around various parts of the Wildlife Management Area without success.

Ultimately the mist changed to a light sprinkle and we slowly made our way back to the Blazer. A downpour commenced moments later and continued with no letup. It was time to go. Wet, cold, no quail and no shots fired, we headed home with two very happy dogs. Still, Hilde had not vindicated herself. Blade had shown no great interest in hunting, but then he had not picked up any scent. But I had learned something: next time ONE dog (**and a gun**).

Chapter 21

The Second Hunt Test

The next available Hunt Test was to be held in Connecticut and we entered Hilde for both days. I was especially excited and looking forward to these two tests after watching her performance a few weeks earlier. Those few days prior to the hunt tests were just plain agony since little preparation could be done.

The two and a half hour drive was easy since we had contacted the sponsoring club the night before and received an approximate start time which allowed for a leisurely trip. Bobbie and I stopped for breakfast along the way and that contributed to a relaxed, casual attitude. There was absolutely no doubt in my mind that Hilde would qualify. The weather was absolutely perfect. The conditions could not have been any better. We arrived early enough to let Hilde loosen up and she quickly shifted into the hunting mode.

We were able to observe several braces depart the starting point and work their way down a dirt road enroute to the bird field. We could even observe their turn toward the bird field before losing sight of them. We could also see the last half of the bird field since it was near the parking lot. This gave me some advance information so that I could concentrate more on Hilde if required. Hilde also observed the braces departing and sensed what might be coming. She was clearly interested, but still relatively calm unless we made any movement toward the starting point. I was no longer concerned about her possible attitude toward her bracemate...Hilde was beyond that petty sort of thing.

On one occasion we had watched a brace travel down the road and eventually disappear into the bird field.

Moments later we heard some frantic whistle blowing and observed one of the dogs from that brace coming toward us along the dirt road. One of the judges for the next brace mentioned that if the dog reached the parking lot that it would be disqualified. Immediately the spectators began yelling for the dog to go away! Do you know anyone who teaches his dog to "go away?"

Observing all of this new attention, the dog happily continued toward the parking lot. He came right up to the edge of the parking lot and suddenly turned and raced away down the dirt road to the applause and delight of the spectators. We saw him turn toward the bird field and disappear. Everyone felt good about this turn of events. Unfortunately, the dog proceeded through the bird field and over to the clubhouse without even regaining contact with his handler. The handler exited the bird field without his dog, embarrassed, but with the sympathy of the spectators. His concern now was to find his dog which had now been collared and was waiting for him.

What if Hilde decided to do the same thing? My confidence evaporated. Once I put on my orange vest and cap, Hilde became more excited and attempted to pull me toward the starting point...that was a good sign, but I was still concerned. Added to that, either my breakfast was not agreeing with me or I was becoming somewhat anxious.

Hilde's bracemate was a male German Shorthaired Pointer (GSP) that seemed totally indifferent to Hilde, but then she wasn't overly impressed with him either. This was a little strange since Hilde usually spent considerable time checking out a new dog. Perhaps she was becoming very serious about this special game of hunting. I introduced myself to the other handler and we were able to discuss our dogs and our own backgrounds. This was not a competition between two handlers or their two dogs. We were both novices and discussed the strengths and weaknesses of our dogs plus our own experience or lack of. Then we genuinely wished each other well. That was the way it should be.

Soon we heard our brace called. A quick brief by the judges and off we went down the dirt road with both dogs loose and hunting. Well, first things first, the GSP needed to answer the call of nature. Not to be outdone, Hilde then did the same and would have won if THAT had been a competitive event! Back to the task at hand with both dogs covering a lot of territory.

We worked our way along the dirt road and since both dogs were working well, we were able to talk with the judges and let them point out those items of interest as they watched the dogs working. At the appropriate location we turned toward the bird field and the talking abruptly ceased. It was time to get serious.

Shortly after entering the bird field, the GSP pointed and flushed a quail which flew from the left side to the right side of the bird field. The GSP took off after it; Hilde initially followed and then stopped. One judge and the handler followed the GSP while the other judge remained with me. At this point Hilde began to concentrate on the left side of the bird field. While ranging off to the left, she decided to depth-check the edge of a mini-swamp. If water is nearby, Hilde will find it and check it out. In preparation for the resumption of her hunting pattern she hesitated and looked at me as if to ask "Go around or right through the middle of the swamp?" At home we use the command "Go around" to move the dogs from one side yard to the other side yard or to maneuver them AROUND the coffee table rather than OVER it. What the heck...maybe it will work out here, "Hilde, go around!" She did. I was surprised, but tried not to show it. The wide-eyed judge smiled, but I knew what she was thinking: "He talks to his dog." Here we go again!

Hilde resumed her usual pattern, covering ground at a very rapid rate. The bird field contained a large number of oak trees and the ground was covered with leaves. Suddenly she picked up a "hot spot" where a quail had recently been and briefly pointed then dismissed it almost immediately. She moved a few feet and then froze in that very special, intense point that leaves no doubt in anyone's mind. I called the point actually feeling foolish as I did so since it WAS so intense. She was trembling with excitement. Remembering the firing problem from the first hunt test, I drew the blank pistol and DOUBLE-CHECKED the cylinder to ensure that the pistol was ready to fire. It would be nice to get the shot off BEFORE the bird LANDED. I approached Hilde from her right, looking for the quail in the thick leaves. I gave her a "whoa" even though I didn't think she needed it. She was incredibly intense and nothing I did distracted her. It was tempting just to stand and stare at her.

Drawing from my vast experience (remember...it was three birds, all flushed at once!), I concentrated my search for the quail about four or five feet in front of her; I couldn't find anything. I was forced to move carefully to avoid some eye-level branches. I stepped back and to the left to avoid one particularly threatening branch. Suddenly the air exploded just behind me as the quail flushed! Startled, I turned further to my left and the pistol went off automatically! I congratulated myself for having the good sense to hit the outhouse (yes, outhouse) immediately prior to the commencement of this brace.

The quail had flushed almost vertically and was probably still recovering from the spinning (a dizzying process that keeps the quail from moving away from its "planted" position for a few minutes). The spinning had occurred immediately prior to the quail being planted. As the bird reached the height of my extended arm, I had fired the pistol and it was only about 2 feet from the already-addled bird. The bird departed the field and I turned toward Hilde and saw her following its flight. I did not receive "the look." That was good, I hate criticism from a dog...even Hilde.

The judge took a moment to mention that Hilde had been less than one foot from the quail and **could** have grabbed it on the ground or when it flushed, but showed amazing restraint. It was obvious that the judge was impressed with this gray dog. This time I had the smile. She told me that she had seen enough and that I could pick up my dog. Hilde and I left the bird field while she waited for the other judge, dog and handler.

Bobbie was literally jumping up and down as Hilde and I approached the parking lot. "Honey, I saw Hilde point and you draw the pistol and then the strangest thing happened!" she exclaimed. She explained how the quail flushed, the pistol fired and the bird flew out of the field and up to the parking lot. There it flew right into the side of a van that was backing out of a parking spot. The dazed quail then moved to a place of safety...right in front of the rear wheel of the van! Frantic spectators yelled for the startled driver not to move forward. One of the judges for the next brace rescued the quail so it could recuperate in safety. Ultimately, the quail was released while a small but happy crowd registered its approval.

Oh, by the way, Hilde qualified with one-half point short of a perfect score and I DID NOT receive "the look" even once. Bring on the next hunt test!

Chapter 22

The Third Hunt Test

Two Hunt Tests and two "qualifieds" for our Hilde...everything was going nicely. The third Hunt Test was the day after and at the same location as the second test. The weather was good, the drive to Connecticut was easy once again and brace number fifteen was perfect timing for us. We even did the breakfast routine again. Everything was going our way and it appeared that this Hunt Test would be a breeze. There was nothing more to wish for and we calmly waited for our brace to be called.

Hilde's performance the day before had been exceptional and I was certainly expecting a repeat. We arrived early enough to simply relax, but Hilde was anxious to get out of the Blazer and move around. After thirty minutes, she was warmed up, ready to go and was forced into the "hurry up and wait" routine. There are limited activities to kill time and it was spent walking around or sitting on the tailgate with Hilde. As our start time approached, I sought out Hilde's bracemate and handler.

Hilde was paired with a German Shorthaired Pointer (GSP) again. Well, what did you expect – the Hunt Test was hosted by a **GSP** club! This time, however, it was a wound-up female. Bobbie really **hates** that OTHER word! Her owner/handler (the DOG, not Bobbie) gave me an extended, running account of his GSP's superior abilities and talent. As if on cue and right before my eyes, that dog started looking toward the bird field and whining. As he continued to brag about his dog, I thought how odd it seemed that most other handlers talked about past or present problems with their dogs. Here was a handler who seemed intent on psyching me out with endless accounts of his dog's talent. In retrospect, perhaps I should have asked him why he didn't start her in Senior or Master instead of Junior.

To make matters worse, his dog started straining at the leash and quivering with anticipation. He made it clear that no other dog could compete with his dog and certainly not a Weimaraner. Just looking at his dog and observing her obvious hunting desire had been incredibly intimidating.

Hilde, meantime, had been looking around for a tennis ball or a toy to chew. This had disaster written all over it! Come on, Hilde, show some enthusiasm! No such luck...Hilde showed absolutely no excitement...and that just reinforced the other handler's case. What a difference from the day before! Any shred of confidence that I might have had just disappeared. Even putting on the required vest and cap had not made a difference in Hilde's demeanor. Was she ill? There was nothing to indicate that she felt bad...she just had no motivation at a time when I really needed her to demonstrate that she was ready to hunt.

Finally, our brace was called. (Okay, Hilde, just go do your thing.) One of the judges briefly touched on rules and the course, asked if we had questions and told us to unleash the dogs. That GSP took off like a shot down the dirt road with Hilde in hot pursuit! (Hello...this is a HUNT TEST...oh what the heck, come on, Hilde, faster! YOU CAN TAKE HER!) After about 100 yards they broke off to the right side and commenced hunting, but Hilde was still competing. We finally caught up with the two dogs and the GSP took the left side of the road so I moved Hilde to the right. It was time to get serious.

Seconds later the GSP slammed into a point along the edge of the road. The handler called it, drew his pistol, flushed the quail and fired. (Jeez, we're not even NEAR the bird field...this could be a LONG day!) Hilde, energized by the sound of the shot, began working really hard off the right side of the road. The two judges and the other handler were discussing this unique circumstance when the GSP **once again** pointed a bird near the edge of the road (a REALLY LONG day!). By this time Hilde was becoming frantic...SOMEONE was having fun but not her. Of course we all know who was REALLY getting frantic! And worst of all, the other handler's obvious overstatements were being realized right before my eyes. Was Hilde really outclassed to the extent he had insinuated? Remember, the dogs were NOT competing against each other, but against a standard...I had to remind myself about that fact. It didn't help at all!

We finally reached the bird field; the GSP was flying and covering most of the width of it. A quick learner, Hilde began to hunt WITH the GSP. Well at least she knew enough to go with a winner! (Wait a minute, whose side are you on?) I called her and tried to move her into her own pattern, but she broke it off and headed toward the GSP and blew past her just as she POINTED AGAIN. (Give me a break!) Hilde continued a few more yards and then reversed course and cut right in front of the still-pointing GSP without registering anything. The judge nearest me glanced my way with a raised eyebrow and I mumbled, "There's nothing there, false alarm." (Good girl, Hilde...we'll discuss the "failure to honor" later.) There was no bird, thank goodness, and the GSP resumed hunting. "I TOLD you so," said a small voice inside of me.

Shortly thereafter, the GSP pointed AGAIN (Ho hum, what else is new?), the handler flushed the bird and fired his pistol. The GSP took off after the bird! (Ha ha, you can't catch it!) It was not easy to contain my glee! The other judge and the handler took off after the GSP. "Tough break," said that same small voice in a sarcastic tone. The perfect dog was chasing the quail! I was suddenly aware that the sun was shining.

"Okay, Hilde, do your thing. Don't go **through** the mini-swamp. Good girl!" She began running her normal pattern and now we had the majority of the bird field to ourselves. Since two quail were planted for each brace, there should be at least thirty of them nearby and at least several extras in the actual bird field. Life was good. Hilde was running crosswind and covering a lot of ground, but still no birds. (ANYTIME, Hilde.)

Over the next few minutes there were three more shots from that same pistol. (Are we using the WRONG bird field? Cheer up, Hilde, I think he's probably out of ammo...wow, that's depressing! Probably has a blister on his trigger finger! He's probably deaf by now. Do you realize how long the ride home is gonna be? This is not fun at all.) "Stop your whining," said the small voice.

With the unsearched portion of the bird field rapidly shrinking, I resigned myself to the probability that this would not be a successful test. Hilde swung close by and hesitated for a second. During that brief time, we made eye contact and as she had done hundreds of times before, she winked at me with her left eye. I know it wasn't a **real** wink, but I was DESPERATE. Above all, I wanted to believe that she was letting me know that everything was under control. (Just one quail, Hilde, just one quail.)

In less than a minute she locked into a rock-solid point and life became wonderful again. I called the point, flushed the quail and fired the shot while Hilde calmly followed the flight of the bird. "Good girl." She looked up at me and there was that "wink" again. Was it a wink? I don't REALLY believe it was, but then, maybe, just maybe....

"Hey, you've still got 5 minutes," said the judge. Hilde resumed the hunt, but we were at the end of the bird field and encountered no more birds. "You can pick up your dog," said the judge. Hilde qualified. "What were you worried about?" asked the small voice.

We purposely waited at the clubhouse for the other handler and his dog even though we were anxious to hit the road for home. He didn't show while we were there probably knowing that I was eager to ask him about his dog's tendency to chase quail. I must admit, though, that his dog was ALMOST as impressive as he had stated, and stated and stated.

Chapter 23

The Fourth Hunt Test

It had been more than three months since the last Hunt Test and we had done essentially no training during that time. Busy schedules and bad weather had stopped the training and practice sessions. Now with the spring Hunt Test cycle starting, it was time to finish the remaining leg of her Junior Hunter qualification. Hilde had just recently returned from an out of state romantic interlude and was probably waiting for the phone call which would never come.

I had already entered her in the next available local Hunt Test. It was mandatory to get her back up to speed. There was no real sense of urgency on my part since Hilde loved this special sport. As a precursor, I decided to get her "psyched up" by using some hunting terms and commands with some special emphasis. Hilde was not the least bit interested in those verbal cues that I had always utilized to increase her excitement about hunting. Between bad weather and a hectic work schedule, I just wasn't able to take her out for some serious practice. Time was running out.

Finally, a few days prior to the test I was able to take her out to a nearby ball field, but that was to be our only practice. I removed her leash and let her run for a few minutes and then called her with a hand signal. She responded immediately and I was certain that things were falling into place very nicely. We warmed up with some basics and then I planted the quail-scented dummy. Hilde was not the least bit interested. Granted, she did locate the dummy, but she would not even pick it up much less retrieve it. I told her to "whoa" and watched her assume her motionless pose. I picked up the dummy and threw it as far as possible. At midpoint in its trajectory I yelled "bang" and waited until it hit the ground. "Go fetch!" Hilde trotted off to the location of the training dummy then turned and looked at me. She had no intention of retrieving it. Retrieving was not required for the junior hunt test, but we always included it in our practice sessions. The fact that she had trotted to the dummy rather than her normal high-speed run was truly a source of aggravation. It was difficult to refrain from fussing at her, but I feared that it might be counter-productive.

Hilde stood there while I approached and I was sure that she would grab it just as I reached for the dummy. Nope. I grabbed the dummy and she immediately tried to take it away from me. We played tug for a minute and I finally wrestled it from her. Then we made a game of it! Perhaps it was the embarrassing sight of her master running around like an idiot or maybe she thought that I was doing the appropriate things, but she responded and suddenly HILDE WAS BACK! We played for more than 30 minutes until it became too dark. She needed just one more "qualified" for her Junior Hunter certificate and I was no longer worried.

The Hunt Test was local and she was entered on both days...just in case. The first day dawned overcast with a moderate wind from the north and a temperature of 22 degrees. The wind-chill factor was so low that I tried not to even think about it. A couple of inches of snow adorned the landscape and that made it look even colder outside. Insulated boots or standard boots? I chose the standard boots and, oh yes, gloves!

We were in the third brace and paired with a nice lady whom we had met at all of our previous Hunt Tests. She had her wound-up Brittany Spaniel who was also on the last leg of her Junior Hunter certification. And speaking of last leg, this lady was on crutches due to a leg/foot injury! This was one tough woman and that was meant as a sincere compliment.

While waiting our turn and trying to stay warm, I

noticed that the Brittany was even more "wired" than normal. Hilde was exceptionally calm and even allowed the young Brittany to run right up to her without so much as her famous killer stare (It had to be the cold).

The Brittany kept eyeing the bird field and went "ballistic" when the "bird planter" departed with the birds. Shortly thereafter the judges indicated that it was time to go. We were a funny collection of humans with two dogs. I had the hood up on my windbreaker with my orange hunting cap on top of that. My partner was better dressed, but those two crutches just looked out of place. No one laughed...it was probably just too cold. And the few spectators present refused to venture from their warm vehicles!

We walked approximately 25 yards down the road and it was time for her to jettison one of the crutches. She also removed a glove and drew her pistol explaining that she would be too busy if she waited until her Brittany was on point. This had something to do with her dog's nasty habit of flushing, catching and eating the bird which is frowned upon in hunting circles. I elected to retain my gloves until entering the bird field.

Moments later it was time to unleash the dogs. I knew where the Brittany would go! (Don't follow her, Hilde.) Sure enough, the Brittany headed straight for the bird field with Hilde right behind her! Luckily we were able to turn both dogs and gain some semblance of order. The dogs began to settle down into basic hunting patterns although the Brittany would still be considered by most to be excessively wound up. Our progress around to the entrance to the bird field was uneventful until just prior to reaching the entry point.

About twenty-five yards before the turn to enter the bird field and just prior to removing my gloves, everything changed! We were walking downwind next to a thin stand of trees on our right. There were hundreds of little clumps of grass showing where the snow had blown away and they vaguely resembled quail, but certainly did not fool the dogs. The Brittany was checking the trees while Hilde ranged mostly off to the left. She was roughly thirty feet out and ahead of us, moving from left to right and approaching the "road" which we were using for our trek. Suddenly, Hilde wheeled to her right and slammed into her solid point facing us! Sure enough, about four feet in front of her was the quail, squatting down but in plain sight in the snow looking almost like a clump of grass.

As my brain deciphered the image (Hallelujah!), the "Brittany from Hell" came out of nowhere and RAN OVER the quail, flushing it! It was hard to determine who was the most surprised: the quail, the Brittany, Hilde or me (or the other handler or the two judges). The timeframe from point to flush was perhaps two seconds. A bewildered Hilde followed the flight of the bird awaiting the shot (And probably planning how to deal with the Brittany when the time came). Immediate apologies flew from the Brittany's handler (interspersed with some acute verbal direction to her Brittany!). I wanted an instant replay since it had happened so quickly.

The judge nearest me told me that if I had gotten off a shot it would have counted just the same as if it had occurred in the bird field. She mentioned that Hilde had pointed and held steady and that NOBODY could have missed THAT point! Lamely, I explained that I could not have removed my glove, drawn and fired the pistol and still felt that I was following the rules. I never mentioned that I was just too dumbfounded to react.

I wasn't the least bit worried, we had not yet entered the bird field and Hilde was obviously very serious and at the top of her game. There were probably one or two quail still in the bird field from the previous two braces plus the two planted for our brace. We entered the bird field with the wind from our right. After about 40 yards, the Brittany pointed a bird and her handler was engaged in arriving quickly (hobbling as fast as her crutch would allow) before the Brittany broke point and had breakfast.

Great, now we can alter our pattern to locate the other quail. Hurry, Hilde! She covered a lot of ground in a short period of time. Nothing, nada, zilch! Suddenly, we heard the sound of a blank pistol shot. Look out, Hilde, here comes you-know-who. Soon both dogs were searching and still nothing. Time expired without locating any other birds. Well, at least the Brittany didn't find another bird. That would have REALLY made my day!

All at once I became acutely aware of how cold my feet were. And my ears ached! And I was hungry. The distance to the Blazer was short, but the trek was long. Walking out next to a lady using a crutch and controlling her new Junior Hunter (AKA, The Brittany from Hell) was devastating to me. My "congratulations" must have sounded hollow while her repeated apologies sounded so sincere. I was truly happy for her, but I don't think it came across well. This was Hilde's first failure to qualify and I regretted postponing the removal of my gloves. Hilde had done her job; I had not done mine. I was certainly glad that I had entered Hilde for both days. Tomorrow would be a better day.

In an effort to cheer me up, the other judge sought me out and, standing in the cold, freezing wind, advised me that if I had simply fired a shot, then Hilde would have qualified. It didn't cheer me up, it DEPRESSED me!

The next day Hilde qualified with ease and with no unusual circumstances. Well, I WAS forced to CHASE the quail to flush it, while Hilde developed her new technique called a MOVING point: four steps, point; four steps, point, etc.

Chapter 24

Two Much

One of the first rules of having dogs is to keep them under control. While Hilde and Blade were well behaved in public, they were far from perfect at home. This was the result of two, and usually three people who enjoyed the excitement of the returning home ritual.

The accepted method is to maintain the upper hand by ignoring the dog or commanding it to behave upon arrival at the home. Allow several minutes to elapse and then acknowledge the dog. This lets the dog know that jumping and wild displays are not acceptable. It also lets the dog know that your arrival is no big deal. Thus the dog is a model of restraint and entering the home is easier and quieter. If necessary, a leash can be utilized and a foot on the leash can be utilized to restrain the dog until time to acknowledge the dog's presence. Boy, does that sound boring!

Hilde and Blade always knew when we arrived. After hearing the sound of any of our vehicles, which they immediately recognized, they anticipated our imminent unlocking and opening of the front door. They would proceed to the sofa and stand there looking for us through the window. On those rare occasions where we were able to drive up without their knowledge, the first vehicle door slammed shut would result in their immediate barking until they recognized us. Thus the stage was set for a great reunion. If outdoors upon our arrival, they rushed to the back door, barked and impatiently awaited the opening of the door.

And so it was that we ruined these two dogs, but oh the glory of it all! Here were two dogs so eager to welcome home two members of their pack. It was complete and unrelenting chaos for several minutes and how could we not allow it? Children have never welcomed their parents in this manner and certainly not with this fervor especially when the total separation was as short as thirty minutes. We loved this ritual and never even considered trying to eliminate it. Well, we DID consider it, but it was just too special to avoid.

There were occasional instances where we suffered bruises and scratches from their claws, but these were a small price to pay for the extraordinary joy of the moment. Since Weimaraners are notorious for utilizing their front feet and since they love to maintain eye contact, there is always the possibility of facial scratches. That is the best reason to curtail this bad habit right from the start. If necessary, we could command them to settle down; we invariably chose not to do so. Their happiness was expressed in complete honesty and with no hidden agenda. It was something like dessert without any calories.

There was also an immediate disclosure of any wrongdoing...the welcome home would be less than exuberant. It was then a simple matter of locating the destruction and asking who had done it. The "evil one" would show remorse (either real or fake) and the "good one" would look directly at the culprit. This shameless betrayal of the villain's identity was never resented by the villain...there was just good old-fashioned honesty. There was always plenty of tail wagging, but the unrestrained chaos was just not there. After-the-fact punishment simply would not work. While both dogs were smart enough to know of the wrongdoing, neither could seem to tie the deed to our expressed displeasure. On the other hand, maybe they did and simply played stupid. Regardless, we could not punish without knowing for certain that the guilty one fully understood. Therefore, there was only verbal punishment which never did any good. Since the wrongdoing occurred during our absence, we always attributed it to boredom. Michael suggested that we set up the camcorder and see what showed up. Then he said, "We will probably find out that they can talk!"

Thus it was necessary to catch them in the act and render swift, appropriate justice. Of course they were both smart enough to not commit the same crime twice in our presence. As time went by they committed less and less mayhem which was certainly good news.

* *

As she grew older, Hilde considered certain items to be hers exclusively. Many toys belonged to her and Blade was forbidden to even touch them. Any item that Hilde held could be retrieved by any human member of the pack by simply saying, "Give!" There was no hesitancy at all. This included any food or treat given to her. Imagine my surprise when she grabbed one of four large steaks from a countertop. I caught her just after she grabbed the steak and she froze when she realized that she had been caught in the act. I walked up to her and told her to "give" and she simply stared at me. I was not concerned about recovering the steak for the purpose of cooking and eating it; I just wanted to remove it from her possession.

I repeated the command several times using a deeper voice each time. That didn't work. I noticed that she had a look of fear and certainly remorse, but she had absolutely no intention of relinquishing her prize. I grabbed the steak and repeated the command. She locked her jaws and refused to release the steak. At no time did she growl or indicate that she intended to resort to violence in order to retain possession...she just would not let go. Finally, I took both hands and attempted to pry her jaws open. I immediately became aware of how powerful her jaws were and after approximately two minutes she released the steak. She then exhibited very clearly that she was sorry and apparently expected some form of punishment. I told her that she was a bad girl and let it go at that.

I was perplexed that she had taken the steak in the first place. Hilde knew the rules and never took food from a countertop. Okay, I can see where perhaps the aroma of the steak was simply too much for her. She had grabbed it when no humans were in the same room, which leads me to believe that it was similar to some of the earlier problems that occurred during our absences. Yet there was one other perplexing thing: why wouldn't she release the steak? That bothered me until I realized that we had not GIVEN the steak to her. Apparently, she assumed that the steak was hers since she had "earned" it by acquiring it on her own. Maybe this was Hilde following instincts derived from thousands of years of canine evolution. Then this could have been her attempt to retain that which was hers. Okay, I wrote that one off to instincts, but I did not allow her to keep the steak.

Blade did not exhibit any similar type of behavior. He was just a big, adorable dog that only required some attention. He had few needs and no demands except for occasional acknowledgment of his existence. Actually there was one odd thing that concerned the television. Blade would intently watch any show that featured any type of cat. From lions or tigers down to house cats, he would watch until that segment ended or a commercial came on. There was no point in trying to interrupt him while any of the cats were in view. At times he would rush to the television to get a better view; you could judge the amount of his interest by the amount of the screen that you had to clean.

There was one other type of program that he loved: bull riding. He would watch the bull riding competition while ignoring bronc riding, steer wrestling and calf roping. I have no idea what made this such an item of interest to him. No one in our household watches rodeo so these have been random events when the television was set on a sports channel which just happened to include rodeo competition.

While we are on that subject, Hilde also had her

television preferences. She was more conventional: she loved dogs of all types. We have several photos of her sitting in front of the television while watching the Westminster Kennel Club show which occurs each February. Any show with a dog would immediately capture her attention. Naturally, the greater the action, the more she liked it. Throw in a hunting show and she would become extremely emotional about it! And of course there are the commercials that feature dogs. There have been several that have Weimaraners in them and they are not any more exciting to her than any other breed...that surprised me.

On the subject of surprises: Hilde once observed Blade place both front feet on a kitchen counter. Immediately she raced into the kitchen and persuaded him to leave the entire kitchen in a manner that was clearly Hilde's trademark. I mentioned to Bobbie that Hilde had just disciplined Blade for violating a house rule. She replied, "Hilde didn't punish him for breaking the rules...she just made sure that he didn't get any of the food on the counter." In retrospect, I think Bobbie nailed that one.

* *

Blade still had not shown a lot of interest in hunting. He loved to run free, but unlike Hilde, chose not to search for game. Actually, that is not quite true. Baby blue jays had landed in the yard while learning to fly. Blade caught two of them in spite of the attacking parents. We feel that he removed them as intruders. The same is true for shrews. Blade has sat near the chain link fence near our neighbors' garden waiting for a shrew to venture into range. It was obvious that he had picked up their scent and refused to move until he had dispatched this latest threat to our safety. It might require mere minutes or even hours, but he would not leave. We should not be surprised, the breed was developed to hunt furry (as opposed to feathered) game in Europe. Thus he was fulfilling his purpose in life, but on a very, very small scale!

While Hilde had been our only dog, she had proven that she could be left alone in the house without doing damage. Obviously this was after she had approached adulthood. The addition of Blade had created a situation where both dogs could not be left alone in the house for other than very brief periods. When Blade reached adulthood, he decided to mark some household items. We tried to put an end to that, but met with moderate success. There are several products on the market that will remove all traces of the marking and we kept a supply on hand. We were unable to catch him in the act which made it even more difficult to cure the habit. Then, without warning, he stopped completely.

Our joy was short-lived when he resumed several months later. He marked only when left in the house after observing Bobbie and me leave. In each case Michael was home, but in his room. This did not occur on a regular basis, perhaps every two or three months. If the weather was decent, we automatically let them go outside and then left. Michael could let them in as long as he remained anywhere except in his room.

Inclement weather, especially rain, created yet another problem. The presence of two dogs further reduced the amount of grass in the backyard. Consequently, when the dogs entered the house, they brought in sand or mud which was mostly deposited on the vinyl flooring in the kitchen. Of course they retained a little for application on carpets and furniture. On one occasion, Bobbie and I were preparing to depart the house and let the dogs in for a quick visit. Hilde immediately jumped up on Bobbie who had not anticipated that possibility. Bobbie looked down and exclaimed, "I've got pawprints all over me!"

Simple problem – simple solution. We placed a beach towel on the kitchen floor next to the doormat with a second towel in reserve. When it was time for the dogs to enter the house, we allowed them in one at a time.

Each dog was detained while one of us wiped their feet and gave them the "okay." In this respect, Blade was the star. All you had to do was say, "Feet" and he would lift his left front paw. When that one had been cleaned, he would lift the right paw. Then he would move up and repeat the process with the other two paws. A simple "okay" and he was on his way! Hilde forced you to lift each foot.

Chapter 25

Territorial Expansion

Hilde had been slow to expand her territory. Initially, she had considered her crate to be her own special piece of property. Soon she included the kitchen and living room. As she grew and as her confidence increased, she included our house on a room-by-room basis until the entire house "belonged" to her as part of her den. The next logical step was the backyard. Since this was a fenced area, we assumed that her territorial expansion was now at an end. We had forgotten our vehicles...she became protective of our two vehicles on those rare occasions where she was left alone in them. She did not mind if people walked nearby, but stopping to look at or visit with her was certain to evoke some serious barking. I was surprised at the number of people that would walk up to a vehicle with a barking dog in it and try to pet the animal. We were able to convince her that some people really did want to visit with her and she began to tolerate that. Of course the windows were open enough that she could stick her head out and watch for our return. She did not whine or bark...she just waited patiently.

With the arrival of Blade and especially after he had grown a little, Hilde became more vocal again. The new puppy brought school children and other small visitors into our yard. Although they only wanted to pet or look at the little puppy, Hilde became either jealous or protective and made it clear that the children were not welcome. We would discourage the barking if we were home, but otherwise Hilde kept up her barking until the children were clearly exiting the yard. It wasn't long before Blade joined Hilde in the barking role. I doubt that he knew why he was barking, but nevertheless the entire front yard became their expanded territory.

Some time after that the two dogs decided that the road in front of the house was also their territory. Neighborhood vehicles were free to come and go without incident; a strange vehicle was guaranteed to trigger the barking routine. The FedEx Man was exempt, but the UPS Man and his truck were not acceptable. It was impossible to quiet either dog whether inside or outside if the UPS Man arrived. We have no idea why. We have no reason to think that anyone from UPS ever created a problem for our dogs although most packages delivered to our house are handled by that company. Sometimes the packages were left considerably short of the front steps!

Anyone else who dared to approach our front door was guaranteed to receive Hilde and Blade's most impressive barks, but nothing like the treatment previously mentioned. Both dogs utilized a very deep bark that sounded far more ominous than their normal barks. No stranger would care to meet what must most certainly be huge monsters lurking behind that front door! Once we acknowledged the stranger, we could command the dogs to be quiet.

At first, Blade never initiated the barking...he simply followed Hilde's lead. By the time he was a year old, he began to commence the barking without any consultation with Hilde, although at a quieter level. Once Hilde joined in he would increase his own volume. Sometimes at night he would hear some mysterious sound and bark. We have surround sound with our television and stereo and even though he could see the source of the sound on the television, the fact that the sound came from the side or from behind was unnerving to him. Usually we could quell the barks by saying, "It's the TV," or something similar and both dogs would immediately relax and go back to sleep or whatever their activities had previously been.

At some point in time, though, Blade chose not to heed our commands to be quiet. He would bark just a little quieter; we would respond with "Quiet." He would then reduce the volume a little more and we would continue with "Quiet!!" Again, he would reduce the volume and would be rewarded with "Quiet!!!" This would continue until he barked at the whisper level and our response was so loud that it became funny. At this point if you listened carefully, you would hear a final "woof" and he would look at you out of the corner of his eyes and then go to sleep, proud of getting in the last word. This was his one overt act of defiance. This seems awfully similar to daughters Debbie and Donna during their teens.

Invasion of Hilde and Blade's territory by other dogs was a concern. The yard fence was only four feet high and either dog was capable of jumping over it without any difficulty. The only reason that they never even tried it was simply that they had been taught that they were not allowed to even try. The occasional stray or escapee that ventured in front of our house would be greeted by a chorus of loud barks. Usually that was enough to encourage the trespasser to depart and normal tranquillity would soon prevail.

The volume of strays and escapees was very small and their appearance was a rare occasion. That made it extremely difficult to keep our two dogs quiet since they would revert to their old ways after a week or so. Two of our neighbors and some occasional summer visitors would routinely walk their dogs in front of our house. Usually both Hilde and Blade could be silenced easily, either by us or by an adult that the dogs recognized. Just speaking their names was usually enough to stop the barking. The real problem was caused by children walking dogs and especially small children with large dogs. Once the barking began, most children did not understand the gravity of the situation. Rather than turn around or continue past our house, they would just stop and stare at the two agitated Weimaraners. This was considered a "challenge" and would aggravate Hilde and Blade. To make matters worse, sometimes the dog on the leash would become somewhat hyper. If the dog on the leash was strong enough, he would drag the child away in his departure or drag the child into the yard if he decided to check out our two barking dogs. On several occasions we had to explain to young children that stopping with the dog and staring at barking dogs was not a good idea. It would have been even better to explain that to the parents along with a caution to not allow small children to walk large dogs.

We are not excluding ourselves from blame since we were not sufficiently aggressive in our attempts to control the barking of our own dogs. Under the right conditions virtually any dog may depart from its normal demeanor and demonstrate aggressive behavior that has been overridden by training or conditioning. The absence or presence of barking may not be sufficient indication of any dog's current mind-set. The situation might also trigger an aggressive response that has not been demonstrated before and which is certain to surprise the owner. The height of our yard fence was definitely not enough to contain the dogs if the right conditions were reached.

Earlier I mentioned that Hilde had shown territorial aggression toward Bailey, the yellow Lab from next door when she visited our yard one day. Months later we were in for a major shock when Bernie took Bailey out for a late afternoon walk with his children, Sarah and Richard. Blade and Hilde were excited and barked, but hushed as the assembly moved on down the road. Both dogs then raced around to the other side yard for a better view and stood on their hind legs with their front paws on the gate. The gate opened! Someone unfamiliar with the latch had apparently exited that gate and failed to push the latch all the way down, a feat requiring a series of steps. We heard the sound of seriously growling and barking dogs and rushed outside. There was Bailey on her back in complete submission with Blade and Hilde standing over her. Hilde seemed to be playing a lesser role and immediately responded to my command to stop, but Blade continued to growl and hold Bailey immobile.

Richard was now on his dad's shoulders and crying while Sarah ran for help. I collared Hilde and then grabbed Blade and took them back to the yard.

Bailey suffered some minor bites, Richard was terrified, Sarah was somewhat frightened and Bernie was bewildered, but calm. Bernie's wife, Carol, soon arrived on the scene and was obviously concerned due to the presence of the children. Bobbie and I were horrified that the incident had taken place and profusely expressed our apologies; good neighbors are not to be taken for granted. None of us could have anticipated this occurrence and it was time for some serious action. We overlooked the fact that someone had entered our yard or at least opened the gate and had not properly closed it. Obviously the gates must be locked at all times, but how could we change the attitude of the dogs?

Blade appeared to be the true aggressor and yet he had never shown this tendency before. Hilde had played a minor role even though she was the "alpha." Apparently she ceased her aggression as soon as Bailey showed submission. Perhaps Blade was in the "pack mentality" mode and was just being a good pack member driven by Hilde's urging. This was a new experience which had been created by Hilde then relinquished and he took over. Bailey was female, well known to both Hilde and Blade and had exhibited total submissive behavior...why would Blade play such an aggressive role? Our timid Blade showing clear signs of aggression? Was this the beginning of a permanent change in Blade? Perhaps Blade enjoyed this new dominance experience. Maybe Blade was beginning a move to unseat Hilde from her position as leader of the canine portion of the pack. That was not the case; Hilde had no intention whatsoever of yielding the throne! Blade would once again receive a quick reminder that Hilde was still in charge.

Chapter 26

Blade and Star in Competition

Once again it was time for the big show at the Bayside Expo in Boston. We had entered Blade in the Best of Breed competition. There was no pressure, just a chance to see how he fared after a layoff. Walking through the huge building, we spotted the show ring area and noticed some crated Weimaraners. Suddenly one of the crates "came alive" with movement which startled Blade and then suddenly he began pulling on the leash to move toward the crate. That was absurd...Blade did not act like that. Seconds later we understood. It was Star and she had recognized Blade. Seconds later he had finally recognized her. What a reunion they had even though it was through the wire crate! Both dogs were so happy. We allowed them to visit for awhile before Sue Thomas appeared and told us to let Star out of her crate. Star divided her time between Blade, Bobbie and me. She had remembered each of us. Even Sue was surprised at Star's memory. That was the best part of the show...the Best of Breed competition was a wash.

There are two small dog shows held in a nearby town each September. We had basically stopped showing Blade except at these shows. This was our way of keeping him in a show-ready condition. Imagine our surprise when Star appeared at the first show. She was now a champion and would be in direct competition with Blade for Best of Breed. I was forced to admit that she looked incredible and there was no doubt that she was THE competition.

Sue allowed the two dogs to greet each other and it was amazing to see them recognize each other. Once again they were excited and it was wonderful to watch them. In the ring, however, it was serious business and Star emerged as Best of Breed and Blade was Best of Opposite Sex. The next day it was a repeat of those same placements. We were not discouraged...Star was simply an exceptional Weimaraner who maintained a position in the top ten of the national rankings. And, she was Hilde's half-sister which made it that much better.

One year later and it was time for the two shows again. We secretly hoped that Star would not be in attendance...she was continuing her winning ways. Of course, we would be delighted to see her again and Blade would be overjoyed. Walking from the parking lot with Blade we wondered if Sue would be there with Star. Moments later we heard our names being called. Sure enough, it was Sue and she had brought Star. We were not able to let the dogs greet each other prior to ring entry. We went through the entire judging process without the two dogs becoming aware of the other's presence. Star took Best of Breed (again) and Blade was Best of Opposite Sex. After exiting the ring, both dogs suddenly spotted each other and celebrated a joyous reunion.

The next day was a repeat of the previous day. Blade had been Best of Opposite Sex four times in his career and all four involved Star as Best of Breed. It did not matter to us and Blade did not care either way. This was probably a good time to retire Blade from the ring.

Chapter 27

Safety Day

Shortly after the incident with Bailey, my oldest daughter, Debbie, called to inform us that a dog had attacked her son, Kyle. His wound required more than fifty stitches. The attack had occurred at a friend's birthday party while Kyle was being shown the family pet. Kyle simply got too close to the dog that was essentially cornered. The bite area was just above his left eye and profuse bleeding was encountered. Ironically, my grandson was concerned that the dog might be put to sleep as a result of the attack. He was not traumatized and even accepted some of the blame. He became somewhat self-conscious of the scar, but did not become fearful of his own dogs or those belonging to others. Likewise, his sister, Kelsey, suffered no ill effects from the incident.

As a result of this situation we combed the Internet searching for data on dog attacks and were surprised at the volume of material. We were amazed at the magnitude of the biting problem (referred to at least once as an "epidemic") and further astounded that many attacks are not even documented. We found statistics relating to human deaths involving certain breeds known for their size and employment as guard dogs. The big surprise was that several smaller dogs had been responsible for the deaths of infants. Other data indicated the effects of the home environment on a dog. There was data on aggression and virtually every other canine behavior imaginable. The seeds of something very special had been sown.

Pilgrim Nuclear Power Station has an annual Safety Day where industry-related vendors and groups present their wares and services. Plant and home safety are stressed along with health and lifestyle issues. Even the local fire department and state police usually provide an exhibit or personnel and equipment. Additionally, several departments from within the plant provide presentations or displays emphasizing the safety aspects applicable to the various work groups. Maximum participation is encouraged and the entire event is usually well received.

I was approached by a fellow employee named Morgan who asked if it was possible for me to give a presentation on pet safety or canine aggression for Safety Day and would I bring Hilde and Blade to stimulate greater interest. Initially, I was offended that Hilde and Blade were used in the same context as "canine aggression." I thought it over until I realized that Blade and Hilde's episode with Bailey had certainly been an aggressive action. Having seen some of the wealth of information available on the Internet, I agreed.

We spent several days locating and downloading information which would ultimately end up as part of the presentation. We collected numerous articles and statistics concerning dog attacks, some very graphic photos and some information on items designed to provide protection from attacks. The various statistics were researched, compared and selected or rejected with some becoming part of the verbal presentation while others became part of some of the displays.

Safety Day arrived and we took our materials out to the plant and set them up in the designated location. We were next to a huge tent which had been erected in a parking lot. We would be conducting our presentation six times with seating for eighty personnel. Two large displays flanked the "stage" which was actually a large table. One display contained the various news articles on attacks while the other held the gruesome photos and special attack preventive items. These displays were intended for browsing both prior to and after the presentations. The table was the stage for Hilde and

Blade as they assisted with some of the "do" and "don't" portions of the presentation. The two dogs would alternate as the featured dog. We used a large crate as their resting quarters.

Thirty minutes had been allotted for all presentations with a few minutes in between for people to move to the next presentation. The volume of information for our presentation required a minimum of twenty minutes without any interruption. That left ten minutes for demonstrations plus questions and answers. We ultimately combined the demonstrations with the presentation and ended up with five minutes for questions and answers...it was not nearly enough. Word spread rapidly and the up-front seats were filled almost as soon as the previous occupants departed. There was standing room only at each presentation. Hilde was in rare form and made the demonstrations both interesting and humorous; Blade was far more reserved and just decided to pose. Keep in mind that the demonstrations included those actions which may trigger an attack by a dog.

Obviously Safety Day was not a good time to have a dog attack (not that any day is) and so audience participation was not allowed...just in case. We were not worried, but just one episode would be a disaster. Neither dog would be off-leash at any time. We had plenty of cool water and treats for the dogs. The stage was set.

I began the presentation with introductions of people and dogs and the events that would (hopefully) transpire during the next few minutes. I then proceeded to explain the pack hierarchy and how it was in place at our home. I mentioned how we had inadvertently done a lot of the right things without knowing why. I also mentioned how we had done some incredibly idiotic things without knowing! This was followed by attack statistics and reference to the photos. I would then describe and demonstrate an aggressive act toward the dog and point out the reaction and how we had conditioned the dogs to accept it. I would also ask for a volunteer with a high threshold of pain to come up and try the same thing, but never got any takers (Of course I was not expecting any, either). We would demonstrate submissive behaviors which could possibly prevent confrontations with strange dogs. I also demonstrated or discussed what to do if encountering a stray dog. After the question and answer period, people were allowed to come up and introduce themselves to the dogs and both dogs just loved it.

On one occasion I demonstrated how punishment is conducted by a senior pack member toward a junior. Hilde was the lucky dog and was placed on her side and held. I told her, "No, no, no" in a quiet, neutral voice and gave her a shake. I then released her and moved to the corner of the table closest to the audience with Hilde on my right and slightly behind. I mentioned that Hilde probably could not understand what she had done wrong and was certain to try and make up for it. I moved on to the next topic and noticed that the audience was shifting their gaze to my right. I turned to see what Hilde was doing and saw her looking up and away from me...and there was nothing there to see. The audience chuckled and I resumed my spiel.

Once again I saw the audience shift their gaze and begin smiling. This time I turned rapidly and caught Hilde trying to lick my neck or ear. She immediately looked up and away again; too late...busted! The audience laughed and Hilde lowered her head in remorse...probably insincere. The audience laughed again. That was it! Hilde was on a roll. She then demanded to receive forgiveness and I was forced to stop and assure her that all was well. The next presentation involving Hilde was even better since she had learned from this one and the audience was treated to more of her antics. Then someone brought out a camera.... Talk about losing control!

Blade, on the other hand, was just there and had no agenda. He looked exceptional that day, and was completely unaffected by the audience. There was one presentation, however, where he inadvertently stole the show. With him on the table and restrained by a short leash, I explained that for some unknown reason both dogs hated the UPS truck and the UPS Man. As if on cue, the UPS truck drove by for the morning pickup at the plant. Blade spotted it before I did and growled slightly. I told him to be quiet and he watched the truck until it disappeared. The audience was clearly amused. We demonstrated some of the other behaviors and Blade demonstrated the actions of a good junior pack member. And then the UPS truck came into view again as it departed! This time Blade was a little more concerned and the audience turned to see why he was so excited. This triggered their laughter again and Blade became oblivious to anything until the truck once again disappeared. He then turned back to the audience and stood a little taller and everyone knew that he was proud of having chased the evil truck away by simply staring at it. I explained that FedEx was considered acceptable to both dogs for some reason and the audience looked toward the road expecting to see a FedEx truck arrive. I actually had to explain that the UPS truck was NOT part of the demonstration!

By alternating the two dogs for the presentations, we felt that one dog could rest and cool down in the shade. Unfortunately, after one cycle the off-going dog wanted to stay in the limelight and whined to come out of the crate. Bobbie allowed it sometimes, but usually had to put the dog back into the crate due to the disruption. Both dogs were clearly enjoying this break in their normal routine.

The question and answer period was incredible each time. The discipline demonstration and the various aggressive/submissive demonstrations invariably brought several individuals to state their total lack of knowledge of these behaviors. Where could they find this information? Was it too late to change the behavior of their dog? Some questions were easily answered and others were far beyond our ability. We tried to channel them toward appropriate sources and reminded them, as we had initially done, that we were novices and that professional help might be required.

Between sessions, there were more questions and requests to pet both dogs. People waited and were often late for the next presentation on their route. Both dogs not only tolerated the attention, they ate it up! Individuals would ask if they were using the right technique to greet the dog rather than take the chance of surprising Hilde or Blade and being bitten. At this stage, neither dog cared how or where they were touched!

I noticed a few people who remained well back instead of coming forward and asked if they were interested in petting the dogs. The response was usually either "I'm afraid of dogs" or "I was bitten once." At least one individual who was afraid of dogs finally ventured forth and petted Blade whose attitude went from neutral to delight...almost to the point of scaring the individual. The change in that individual from what I am certain was genuine fear to confidence that Blade would not cause any harm was quite a spectacle. Blade seemed to sense the initial fear and essentially froze except for his tail which was wagging so hard that his entire body shook. He had somehow noticed her fear or discomfort and apparently the wagging tail was her signal that he was not about to harm her in any way. This particular individual ultimately allowed Blade to sniff her quivering hand and eventually stoked his head. He responded with gentle pressure against her hand and her transformation began. I told her to rub his neck and when she reached the right spot, Blade made it very clear that he was now her slave! What a ham! She eventually petted him from head to toe and he showed his appreciation, but without getting too rambunctious. I am certain that he would have left with her and I think she would have taken him. That one incident made all of the long hours of preparation worth it. Hilde would not have been acceptable under the same circumstances since she does not feel the need to impress anyone. She would have tolerated the woman's touch, but would not have conveyed the message that she enjoyed the petting.

Eventually, the final presentation was completed and the last question and answer session came to an end. We were amazed at the amount of interest in the information which we had provided. We were also surprised at the interest in the two dogs. Many people from the plant had seen one or both dogs when I did some of their training out at the plant during late afternoons or on weekends. Many other personnel had not seen a Weimaraner up close and were anxious to ask about the breed. We always provided the pros and cons even though we were somewhat prejudiced. From our point of view, the presentations had been a resounding success.

Blade and Hilde had enjoyed themselves and were not especially eager to return home. The next morning they were ready to do it all over again and remained underfoot until finally deciding that it wasn't going to happen.

Chapter 28

The Grandkids

The second week of December, 2000 was a special occasion. My youngest daughter, Donna, her husband, George, plus daughters Lexie and Taylor came to visit for a week. Lexie was twenty-two months of age and Taylor was six months old. This was their first visit to our home and this would be their first encounter with the two dogs. We had already discussed the possibility that Hilde and Blade might resent this intrusion by four strangers. We were not particularly worried, but knew that a certain amount of caution was necessary. There would be no occasions where the children were left unsupervised with the dogs.

Our guests arrived relatively late at night and we immediately placed the dogs in their crates so that we could greet everyone and unload their minivan with minimal obstruction. We quickly completed that task and by then both dogs were anxious to come meet the new arrivals. They were not going to be ignored and it was obvious that life would be tough until they were allowed to checkout the strangers. We initially used their leashes just in case either dog got too excited. Donna and George passed the initial screening by both dogs with flying colors. And then it was time to greet the kids.

Although Hilde and Blade had been around small children several times, this extended visit would be a real test of their acceptance of small children. Lexie was extremely mobile and was anxious to play with both dogs; Taylor was not very mobile and was not expected to pose any problems. The dogs were extremely curious about both girls and made their constant presence known while we visited. Lexie was showing a growing desire to play with the dogs, but we were reluctant to allow it so soon. Taylor watched the dogs while reserving judgment on them. We visited until we were one the verge of collapse and finally went to bed. We were rudely awakened at dawn by two dogs who were eager to greet their new friends. Oh well, who would really want to sleep late on the weekend after staying up late??

Both dogs ate their breakfast and went looking for the girls. Ultimately Lexie and Taylor appeared, but were still sleepy. Hilde was curious about the girls, but remained just out of their reach. Blade was fascinated and perhaps a little shy around Lexie, but was extremely interested in Taylor. If she was in her jump chair, Blade stationed himself close by and watched her. Apparently he had intentions of guarding her. On one occasion, Hilde walked between Blade and Taylor. Blade immediately made it clear to Hilde that she must never do that again! This was the only time that I have ever seen Blade challenge Hilde and Hilde was only too happy to comply with his obvious demand for her to move. She did not make that mistake again! Blade was also protective of Lexie, but not to the same extent. Perhaps he instinctively knew that Taylor was more helpless.

Both children took their naps in our den which doubled as a bedroom. The door was left open so that we could hear the girls when they awakened. Blade positioned himself on the living room sofa and took a nap. Every twelve to fifteen minutes he would get up, stretch and walk to the den. He would check the playpen and the crib and, satisfied that both girls were okay, return to the sofa and resume his nap. He repeated this procedure every day. When either girl awoke and whether she cried or just babbled, Blade immediately rushed to the den, checked the girls and then sat in the hallway by the den door and softly barked his special bark which means basically "Come here, I want some attention." Upon arrival of any adult, he would precede them into the room and indicate which child had awakened, although that adult could usually figure that out.

Hilde was not the least bit concerned about the welfare of the two girls. She showed no resentment whatsoever, but was perfectly content to let Blade do the worrying. We had expected just the opposite reactions from the two dogs. Obviously Hilde's maternal instincts did not extend to Lexie and Taylor.

On the third day, Hilde was reducing a rawhide "chewy" to slime when Lexie abruptly walked up to her and took it out of her mouth. It happened so quickly that neither Bobbie, Donna nor I could move or even warn Hilde to be gentle! Nothing happened. Lexie looked at the "chewy" and gave it back to Hilde who very carefully removed it from Lexie's hand. None of us could speak for several long seconds. Donna thought nothing of the incident...Bobbie and I almost had heart failure! It was apparent that Hilde recognized Lexie neither as a threat nor as someone who would keep her "chewy."

Lexie pulled their ears and tails, used them for pillows and played with their toys...these were great playmates. Taylor locked her very small but vice-like fingers on their ears or whatever she could grab and never generated so much as a yelp from either dog. On the other hand, both dogs were always available to provide face or hand washing, especially after a meal...that was something we had to watch out for! Actually, they were always available to assist with anything involving the kids and food. The big surprise was that neither dog even attempted to take any food from either girl. Another surprise was that neither dog attempted to avoid the kids at any time.

Eventually Blade and Hilde began to bring their own toys to Lexie apparently hoping that she would play with them. Lexie would grab the toy to examine it and the dog would pull the toy away. After several attempts, both dogs learned to pull just hard enough to keep the game going. Lexie would laugh and shriek with delight which would encourage the dogs to renew their efforts. It was incredible how both dogs accepted the differences in strength and reduced their advantages accordingly.

Bobbie and I were in constant awe of the ability of both dogs to instantly adjust to the play situation; neither George nor Donna could truly appreciate what we were observing.

As Lexie grew more and more fond of Hilde and Blade, she began to imitate them. She began crawling instead of walking...this seemed to please both dogs. Lexie must have sensed this and after watching them drink some water, she took her turn! They allowed her full use of the bowl which happened so fast that none of us could prevent it. Lexie suffered no ill effects and the drinking policy was changed! I do wish that my camera had been readily available!

George was enjoying a leisurely pace except during the mandatory visits to the various items of interest in the local area. While relaxing, he would call Hilde or Blade over to pet them. Both would comply and then walk away. I explained that Blade would soon consider him a good friend, but Hilde would never become his buddy. On day three I was walking to the kitchen when George told me to look and there was Hilde sound asleep with her head in his lap. The shocked look on my face gave George the ammunition that he needed and I received a tremendous amount of good-natured ribbing for several days. There was obviously something about George that Hilde liked and the fact that she felt that comfortable around him was certainly a good sign. Of course, Blade and George were good friends on the first day...Blade's only requirement is a pulse!

Eventually, it was time for our company to depart for Oklahoma. Both dogs seemed on edge in anticipation of some forthcoming change. Having been on many trips themselves, they knew that the packing ritual was an indication of an imminent departure. I don't think they knew WHO was going, but they did know that somebody was about to depart. They watched the loading of the minivan and then carefully watched Bobbie and I for signs that we might be leaving.

The farewells were extended to include Hilde and

Blade and they watched with us as the minivan departed with their newest friends. They continued to watch for their return during most of the day before finally giving up.

Chapter 29

The Last Litter

Hilde was still responsible for providing a second litter in order to fulfill the conditions of the co-ownership agreement with Sue Thomas. A series of schedule conflicts had resulted in a second breeding that occurred late in Hilde's cycle. The pregnancy had appeared to progress normally except that ultimately she was overdue by several days. She had gained more weight than she should have even though we tried to keep her at optimum weight throughout the gestation period. We had assumed that she was carrying a litter of several pups. Unfortunately, she produced a single puppy which was stillborn. We were disappointed, especially since Hilde had to endure the entire process and it would require another breeding.

The next breeding (ten months later) was free of schedule conflicts and came off without a hitch. When Hilde returned from Camelot she resumed her regular routine and life returned to normal for all of us. We were especially watchful of her weight having been fooled by the previous pregnancy. This pregnancy was uneventful and seemed to pass much more quickly than the previous ones. We delivered her to Camelot on a Sunday in April and picked up Star as Blade's playmate. Star and Blade were overjoyed! Star settled in very nicely and our major concern was keeping her weight right where it was. She was doing exceptionally well in the show ring and was scheduled for shows the following weekend.

We received the phone call from Sue on Wednesday. There were nine puppies, six females and three males. Hilde was fine although the first puppy had been a breech presentation. The puppies were all doing well and Hilde was being a good mother. We were ecstatic! But there was more.

Since the puppies require almost constant human supervision, Sue had toyed with the idea of skipping the weekend shows. However, given Star's excellent performance in the show ring, she was reluctant to do so. Would we be interested in raising the litter? That was a heart stopper! Did we want to do that? We thought it over for at least ten seconds. Sure, we could do that. Thus we received a telephonic overview of what we would be doing for the next seven weeks.

Sue would provide us with a whelping box which would serve as home for the puppies until they outgrew it. She would also provide a heating unit and various blankets, pads and other paraphernalia necessary for the care and comfort of the litter. There would be pens and food for the growing pups. And best of all, she would provide the nine puppies and, of course, Hilde. Tail docking and dewclaw removal would be accomplished prior to delivery of the pups to us. Could it get any better?

Since Star was entered in the Saturday show, we agreed to meet at the show site and make the swap there. That would equalize the burden on both parties. Sue would also provide detailed information on all items of concern. So far so good.

We arrived at the show location in Warwick, Rhode Island earlier than required so that the exchange could be accomplished without rushing. I took Star for a walk so that she could stretch her legs and accomplish anything else that needed doing. Sue arrived soon thereafter and we rushed to see Hilde and her brood. Hilde was in plain sight, but the puppies were in a basket to ensure their warmth. We quickly set up the whelping box in the Blazer and loaded all of the other items. I could not believe how much stuff there was!

We piled it on, shoved it in and stacked it up until everything was in place except for the puppies. We loaded Hilde into the Blazer and then added the nine puppies. Sue mentioned that they should be hungry and that now would be a good time for them to nurse. Sue gave us some final advice and directions, grabbed Star and left for the show ring. We were on our own! At that time I think we finally realized just how immense this new responsibility was and how much confidence Sue had in our abilities.

With that sobering thought, Bobbie and I began the process of carrying out our new responsibilities. First of all, we needed to move the Blazer and thus we decided to hit the road. We were forced to turn the heater on and operate it at a high setting to maintain the puppies' body heat. Young puppies cannot regulate their body temperature and that task was now ours for the next several days. Of course that meant that we would be extremely uncomfortable. We were hungry and stopped to eat at a nearby fast food restaurant. There I was able to ensure that the puppies could nurse and fill their bellies. Hilde was absolutely perfect throughout this and soon all nine puppies were asleep. I moved them into their new "basket" and covered the top to avoid any chance of a draft. We continued on our way and light traffic allowed us to make the drive smoothly and safely.

Upon arrival at home, we unloaded the critical items in record time and soon had the whelping box set up in the den and the heater on. Next we added the puppies and Hilde joined them; they were hungry again. We moved everything around so that we knew where each required item was. Finally, we were able to sit back and enjoy the sight of Hilde tending to her litter. I do mean SIT because the heater was required to maintain warmth at floor level which meant that it was much hotter if you stood.

Blade knew something strange was going on and was very curious about the strange happenings in the den. Hilde informed him that she would ruin his life if he chose to enter the den. He really wanted to see what was going on, but Hilde had clearly made him understand that she was serious. After a couple of hours we enticed Blade to enter while Hilde nursed the puppies. He was clearly worried, but the sight of Hilde lying on her side gave him courage. He looked at the puppies and showed great interest until Hilde somehow convinced him to leave. All she did was lift her head!

Everything had stabilized and we could relax. We grabbed the cameras and took some photos. Then we went over our written directions. Each puppy was identified by a colored ribbon around its neck. We had a list of their birth weights and our job was to weigh each puppy and ensure that the lightest ones were allowed extra nursing opportunities and that all puppies continued to increase in weight. The "pink" puppy was the runt of the litter and received the most extra care.

In most cases weight gain was steady, but there were brief periods where there was little or no increase in weight. Adjustments were made as necessary. We knew that a young puppy's health can deteriorate in a hurry, so we constantly monitored them. That first night would be a real challenge. We anticipated little sleep since Hilde had already demonstrated that she would periodically lie down on top of a puppy. Usually she would move enough to allow the pup to crawl free. At other times the puppy might end up behind the pig rail and unable to find a place to nurse...it wasn't dangerous, but the cries were enough to bring us on the run. Most of the night saw either Bobbie or me getting up and rushing to the aid of a puppy in distress only to have the situation corrected by the time we arrived. Walking into that room was a shock since the air temperature at head height was probably one hundred degrees, possibly more.

At approximately 5:30 A.M. on Sunday morning there was yet another distress cry. I heard Bobbie mumble, "I'll go" and I was only too happy to avoid an argument over that. I vaguely remember a groan moments later followed by a noise I did not recognize. I asked what had happened and Bobbie said that she had fallen. I then asked if she was okay and she said, "No."

I rushed to the den and observed Bobbie resting on the day bed and asked if she was injured. She was rubbing her right wrist and said that her elbow and right shoulder hurt. She explained that she had rushed into the room and was somewhat disoriented. In addition, the heat had been too much for her. She had then fallen forward toward Hilde and the puppies. In a desperate attempt to avoid them, she had extended her right hand to avoid falling into the whelping box. Her right hand contacted the smooth pig rail and slid toward the back of the whelping box. A split second later her elbow slammed into the top of the outer side wall of the box. She was hurt, but Hilde and her puppies were uninjured.

I asked her to see if she could move her arm and she replied that she was unable. She said that the pain came from her shoulder and wrist and from her elbow if she attempted to move it. She wanted to just wait for a few minutes and see if the pain would subside; it wouldn't. I asked if she wanted to go to the emergency room and she declined. Less than an hour later she embraced the idea of a trip to the hospital. We left Michael (actually Hilde) in charge and proceeded to the local hospital. It was Easter morning. Well, at least the emergency room would not be crowded. Wrong!

We returned home several hours later with a half-cast on Bobbie's broken elbow. Suddenly we had extra worries to deal with. Bobbie is right-handed and, of course, it was the right elbow that had the fracture. I will not go into great detail, but that created some very special problems. She notified her supervisor of her injury and mentioned that she would not be working for a few weeks. (Think about it: employee states that she will be raising a litter of puppies and will pick them up on Saturday. She then calls two days later to say that she broke her elbow and will be out of work for several weeks...VERY suspicious.) And speaking of suspicious, do you think that the hospital staff believed her story that she had fallen into the whelping box while trying to rescue a puppy? They went to great lengths to keep us apart just in case it was a domestic violence issue! I received numerous angry stares without realizing what was going on.

Bobbie had been working half-days and I had planned to take some time off until the puppies were a little larger. Thus the broken elbow turned out to be a blessing in disguise in a strange sort of way. Bobbie would now be home and keeping an eye on the puppies during these critical first weeks.

The first few days were spent monitoring weights and making sure that the smaller pups were allowed extra nursing time. We also learned that the identification ribbons occasionally came off and needed to be replaced immediately to avoid the possibility of losing the identities of those pups if more than one ribbon were to come off. The best news was when we were forced to change the ribbons since that meant that the puppies were growing. We had nine different colors of ribbon and managed to run out of the spares that Sue had provided. We bought more and kept the process going.

Blade was going nuts during this time. He heard the little grunts, squeaks and occasional yelp and always ran to the door of the den. If Hilde was outside, he might take a quick peek, but usually he just stood at the door and tried to look in without attracting Hilde's attention. On some occasions we were able to let him observe a puppy up close and he appeared to be somewhat frightened.

Puppies have extremely sharp claws that grow rapidly. While nursing, the puppies use those razor-like claws for maneuvering and scratch the mother. This invites infection which can be a disaster. Thus clipping those claws is a constant activity and with nine puppies it is quite a drill. The claws on the hind feet do damage to any type of bedding which is usually an old blanket. Puppies push with the hind legs to move forward or just to maintain their position as they nurse. As they slowly shred the blanket, they produce great quantities of fuzz which requires removal on a continual basis.

At roughly two weeks of age their eyes were open and the bright blue color was just incredible. It was not long before their vision enabled them to actually see and then respond to sight in addition to smell. A week later their hearing became a new sense, but at first it was just a sensation. As they began utilizing these new senses, we could see a distinct change in all of them. They could regulate their own body heat now and not depend on the heater. Hilde had previously been able to sneak into the whelping box; that was no longer possible. At some point the puppies began standing and were soon walking. Actually, they were waddling. As their motor skills improved, they became more playful and engaged in constant battles since their teeth were now in evidence.

These last changes had occurred in rapid succession and every day seemed to bring something new. It was time to move them to their new location, a pen which had been set up in the dining room. We had put down plastic sheeting covered by special rugs with rubber backings. The closest portion of the pen was covered with multiple layers of newspapers. Sue had told us to obtain all of the newspaper we could find; we had not heeded her advice...a week later we were begging for newspapers!

The pen was approximately six feet wide and seven feet long. I had attached a section of hardboard that had a lowered section so that Hilde could jump in and out as necessary. We learned to tape the newspaper together and insert it under the sides of the pen while distracting the puppies. Otherwise, nine puppies would immediately attack the newspaper and it would be impossible to tape the sections together. Of course there is nothing like fresh newspaper to convince a puppy to eliminate and so we invested in huge packages of table napkins in an attempt to extend the life of the fresh newspaper.

It was also time to change the diet of the puppies. Since they had teeth, they could begin transitioning from milk to gruel and then to solid food. This action was applauded by Hilde as a matter of self-preservation. Sue had provided feeding dishes which strongly resembled metal cake pans. We were forced to use two initially with four pups at one and five at the other. Of course the puppies moved around and sometimes all were trying to eat from the same dish. We had also introduced them to water and they went to great lengths to put all manner of things into the water dish. The water required constant changing in the early stages.

Sue had also provided some toys. Some were store variety and some were simply knotted socks. Some of the toys had squeakers and had been specially chosen because the squeaker could not become dislodged. Those were the favorite toys until one of the pups tried to run away pulling a sock. That did it! That became the rage in puppy games. Those squeaky toys had been well received, but chewing on a sibling was more fun. This began to be a common theme after the tug of war games involving the socks.

The individual personalities were becoming evident. Bringing in the food was quickly realized as a human thing even though Hilde was still the preferred supplier. Hilde, on the other hand, was glad to spend less time nursing and was often content just to observe the pups. Any movement toward the pen by a human resulted in all puppies rushing to the edge of the pen. Good things were becoming associated with humans. Although the first few barks were startling to the barker, that was quickly replaced by more and bolder barks. Nine puppies can do a lot of barking! Since barking usually resulted in at least one human arriving, the pups soon learned how to summon a human.

Blade was now able to view the puppies up close and Hilde did not seem to care. He was curious, but was not comfortable around them. We were not concerned that he would harm them...he just seemed to be overwhelmed. He never attempted to jump into the pen, but quickly raced to the pen if he heard a puppy in distress.

The growth continued and the puppies began to move

more quickly. Soon it took three food dishes and we put three puppies at each dish. That arrangement lasted for a few seconds until they could sort out their own ideas. Usually each dish contained at least one puppy standing with all four feet in the dish. This was no concern...Hilde was always ready to clean the pups! They began to consume more water and use more newspaper. Now they absolutely attacked the paper and it was extremely difficult to remove the old paper and replace it. They could anticipate this new game and it became quite a challenge since they knew what to expect.

On warm days we could move the pen outdoors and utilize the kennel to give them a much larger area. At other times we would let them out to explore the entire backyard. Nine puppies can be difficult to keep tabs on, but it was pure joy to watch them play. As if on cue, they would simultaneously become tired and pile up together for a nap. They had also become possessive of special treasures that they found: small branches, pine cones, leaves, etc.. We tied string to an old sock and pulled it around. Some pups would chase or stalk the sock immediately, others took a little more time. They would pounce on it and if they caught it, pulled with surprising strength. We did other tests to evaluate their intelligence and problem solving abilities. Most of the puppies demonstrated the ability to establish a point when exposed to a "bird."

The last two weeks that all nine puppies lived with us was the most rewarding. The time-consuming and never-ending work was offset by the rewards of observing their changing abilities and their genuine affection for their human guardians. Bobbie once stretched out on a blanket in the backyard and was soon laughing as nine puppies attempted to play "king of the hill." They preferred this activity to exploring the yard and soon became tired. Within a few minutes all nine were sound asleep either next to or on top of Bobbie.

The "pink" puppy was the runt and she was such a joy. She had received additional handling and had developed complete trust in her human friends. She was simply a very special puppy for so many different reasons. I now understand why some prospective owners seek out the runt of the litter. The "blue" puppy had been the smallest male and had also received extra handling. He was especially friendly and also had complete trust in his human friends. He was content to simply rest in the crook of your arm or on your lap on his back. The "black" puppy was the largest male and was the first to demonstrate every puppy behavior. None of the other puppies could compare to him. All of the early indications pointed to him as THE pick of the litter. The "red" puppy was the first of the females to demonstrate the expected puppy behaviors. She was always the instigator of mischief. These four puppies were the ones who were most impressive, but for different reasons. The others were in the middle of the group with neither multiple good nor lesser characteristics.

The "black" puppy was selected by his new owner from photos and a description of his special traits. He was to be named Shakespeare and would travel extensively with his new owner. The others were chosen by their new owner as "first pick," "second pick," etc. in order of their deposit submission.

We were contacted by a young couple who had "last pick" which is not really a "pick" at all. Donna and Dave wanted a female and wanted to see all six even though they would receive the one that nobody chose. (That sounds really sad.) They requested a visit and so we invited them over whereupon they promised to only stay for fifteen minutes. Since they were making a three-hour drive, we assured them that they were welcome to stay longer.

Upon their arrival, all six female puppies were waiting in a pen in the front yard. They played with all six and then helped us move them into the backyard with the remaining three males. They thoroughly enjoyed that experience. We discussed the traits of each puppy and stated that the "black" puppy and the "pink" puppy were already spoken for. They asked which one we were going to keep and we mentioned that we had narrowed it down to "red," green," or "beige." They departed and promised to let us know which one they would eventually receive.

A few days later we spoke to Sue and made arrangements to meet with her to transfer eight of the pups to her. We had yet to decide which one to keep and time was running out.

Chapter 30

Mental Telepathy

Blade always imitated Hilde's actions. If she barked, he also barked even if he had no clue why he was barking. If she ran somewhere, he was right behind her. He was learning how she did certain things and incorporated those which were to his benefit; he ignored those things which were of no benefit to him and rejected those which caused Hilde to reprimand him.

They both used the "I want the toy you have" scam on each other with good success, but both dogs would fall for it over and over apparently without learning from it. Surely they were smart enough to recognize this ploy which they used on each other regularly. On the other hand, maybe they used it as a simple diversion from their daily routine. Perhaps they did it just to witness our reaction. Regardless, each dog carried out his/her role without hesitation and the results were always the same...the dog with the toy always lost it to the other and there was no disagreement. Even when Blade (as the most junior dog in the pack) obtained the toy from Hilde (his superior in the pack), she would allow it to occur without ripping him to shreds. Any other such transgression would be dealt with quickly and with predictable results! How did Blade know that this was always a pain-free game? There were other items, too.

An opportunity to go somewhere was always the most wonderful reward possible. Both dogs had been to numerous shows and absolutely loved to travel. The simple act of picking up a leash would drive them both into a frenzy. While that is no surprise to any dog owner, keep in mind that the purpose of picking up the leash may have been simply to move it to another location.

That was not easily communicated to Blade and/or Hilde as they prepared for this new adventure. Of course the leash may have been picked up to take the dogs for a walk in the neighborhood...they were certainly up for that! Then, finally, maybe it was picked up to lead them to the Blazer and a ride to places unknown. Since these occurrences involve sight, there is no surprise to the reaction produced by picking up the leash.

Now let's take SIGHT out of the picture. Some of our leashes have a short section of chain which makes varying levels of noise as they are moved and the dogs can certainly hear the sound and they know immediately what it is and what it could mean. The other leashes are nylon and are virtually silent. Normally these leashes are kept in the hall closet and that door probably has a unique sound that the dogs recognize. We open that closet door regularly without touching the leashes and never elicit even a raised head from the dogs much less an investigation; however, just touching a leash will guarantee two excited dogs ready for some adventure! I don't know how they do it. But it doesn't stop there.

Both dogs know that certain words mean that they are soon to embark on an exciting journey of some sort: "go," "ride" and "out" will generate unbelievable excitement. Those words used in a sentence will trigger this excitement even though it does not apply to the dogs. To combat that problem, we tried to avoid those terms and even tried spelling the words just as you would around a small child. It doesn't matter...when you spell "go" they hear the "o" and figure it out. The same is true with "ride" and somehow they deciphered "out." Since the "o" in "out" is pronounced the same as the "o" in "go," the end result is the same. They do not, however, get it confused with "snow." Are they really that intelligent? I honestly don't think so.

This is where it becomes even more perplexing. On some occasions we might be taking just one of the dogs. Often Hilde or Blade would be asleep on the sofa in the living room while the other was asleep in the bedroom.

Whispering quietly in the ear of either dog will have the other dog wound up and ready to go within seconds. How can a dog that is sound asleep react to that quiet whisper? If the first dog were to jump up and become excited then I could understand that the news was passed by sound and the other dog was checking it out. If there were visual contact where one dog could see the reaction of the original dog, then I could understand that. Mental telepathy...I don't think so.

Next comes the subject of treats. Again, should you attempt to give a treat to one dog without the other knowing...forget it. Same scenario as before, two separate rooms. A piece of soft cheese offered to one dog and eaten without appreciable sound results in the other dog waking up and racing into the kitchen for its own treat. I could follow that if we had provided a crunchy treat or had made a big production out of it by withholding the treat. How do they do it? Mental telepathy...I don't really think so.

Hilde produced a nine-puppy litter in April, 2001. The details are covered elsewhere except for one unusual incident. Since we were keeping one female puppy from that litter, we were observing the females very carefully. Three days before the eight remaining puppies were to be taken to the breeder for disbursement to their new owners, we observed something which was and is still truly puzzling.

We made a habit of handling every puppy the same amount. We referred to them by the color of their identification ribbon and exposed them to as many different situations as possible. This was to see which ones showed early problem-solving abilities or other actions which identified them as fast learners, etc.. We were leaning toward a certain female puppy based on several criteria. The "red" puppy was the first female to walk, run, rear up on her hind legs, point, stalk and pounce. We valued these early indicators above her potential as a show dog and she had one other endearing feature...she was missing a nipple just like Hilde. There was one last factor which was purely a random event: Hilde wears a red collar except when hunting. So it appeared that fate plus our own requirements were pushing us toward the "red" puppy. We did not make that final decision until we met with Sue Thomas for the puppy swap. The "red" puppy was not Sue's recommendation since she was promoting the show ring possibilities while we went with the emotional aspects. The final decision was made at the last minute at the rendezvous point. Up until that point, we had made a conscious decision to treat all nine puppies exactly the same.

On the trip home, with the new puppy (Eva) on her lap, Bobbie commented on the fact that three days prior Hilde had begun disciplining ONLY Eva. I had observed the same thing plus one additional item. Even though Hilde had stopped producing milk, all puppies would attempt to nurse if Hilde was available. Hilde would not allow Eva to nurse; all other puppies were allowed the opportunity.

When we arrived home, Hilde sniffed Eva, looked around for the other puppies and accepted the fact that only Eva was there. There was no mourning. Eva immediately attempted to nurse and was very clearly informed that nursing was not tolerated. There is no doubt in my mind that Hilde somehow knew beforehand that the "red" puppy was our choice AND SHE KNEW IT THREE DAYS IN ADVANCE! Coincidence? Did she hear us say that "red" was the front-runner and understood? Was there something about the "red" puppy that she just did not like or especially did like? Was the "red" puppy just too much like Hilde? Was it simply that our responses to each individual puppy were observed and remembered by Hilde?

Donna and Dave were the couple who came to see all six female puppies even though they would receive the one that was not chosen by anyone else. We did not mention our plans for naming our puppy; Bobbie had picked the name *Sadee*. Donna contacted us several days after our visit and mentioned that they had received the "beige" puppy, which had been one of our three choices. Donna then dropped the bombshell: they had named her *Sadie*! That added a little "Twilight Zone" atmosphere!

Michael's friend Shannon enjoyed taking Blade for walks along the cranberry bogs near our home. This was a special treat for Blade and he was always eager to go. On one occasion, Shannon phoned Bobbie and asked if she could take Blade out for a walk. Immediately, Blade began to show signs of excitement and soon was looking out the window in eager anticipation. His name was never mentioned by Bobbie and it was doubtful that he could hear Shannon's voice over the phone. He knew, somehow, that Shannon was on her way and would be taking him for a walk. If he could not hear the conversation, how could he possibly know? This was not a regularly scheduled event and the phone call was not part of some normal daily routine. He waited for twenty minutes for her arrival, knowing with great certainty what great treat was in store for him. How did he know?

Mental telepathy...dog-to-dog and dog-to-human...I just don't have an answer. Is it possible? Up until now I would have scoffed at anything so preposterous; now I am not so sure.

Chapter 31

Eva – Part 1

Eva captured our hearts immediately. We had watched her as she progressed from a small ball of hair that could neither see nor hear to a larger, much more active miniature of her mother. She was the second one in the litter and the first of the female puppies to demonstrate various levels of achievement. She was the first female to walk rather than crawl. She barked before the other girls. She was the first female to stand on her hind legs and look out from the puppy pen. Best yet, she was the first of the six females to chase, pounce and point. She was bold and extremely active. She was also missing a nipple from the same location as her mother. It was almost as if Hilde had been cloned. Michael was allowed to name her.

On Mothers' Day I was taking pictures of the puppies and stepped into the puppy pen located in the dining room. Hilde was nursing the puppies when Eva (then simply known as the "red puppy") moved up near Hilde's head and laid down face to face with Hilde. Just as I prepared to snap the shutter, Eva moved both front paws to caress Hilde's face. This incredible display of eye-to eye contact must have lasted at least a full minute which led me to believe that this was not a random movement. This was a form of non-verbal communication of some importance. I was able to capture that image and I still marvel at the photo.

Ultimately, Eva stayed and her eight siblings left for their new homes. Eva never seemed to miss them, but then her mother was always nearby. Hilde and Blade had come to our house at ages ten weeks and eight weeks respectively. That was their last contact with their mothers. While their mothers had taught them many things in their brief lives together, we ended up training them in a completely different manner and with varying levels of success. Blade received the better training since we had learned so much from our mistakes with Hilde.

Hilde continued Eva's training on a daily basis. It was incredible to watch her coax or discipline using the smallest possible level of influence. However, greater emphasis was always utilized when necessary! On one occasion Eva decided to chew on the dust ruffle of the love seat. I caught her in the act and grabbed her while saying, "No, no, no!" Hilde was there almost instantly and escorted Eva to another location and commenced to play with her. In a matter of minutes Eva was back chewing on the dust ruffle. Hilde arrived before I could react. Eva was immediately on her back with Hilde all over her and growling far more than she had ever done with Blade. Eva never chewed the dust ruffle or any other part of the love seat again! I have no doubt that Hilde made it perfectly clear that the love seat was off limits for chewing; she had done in one brief lesson what I could not do. The fact that Hilde did this on her own was especially rewarding to me. In retrospect, Hilde had severely chewed the dust ruffle on our other sofa five years prior!

Shortly after she reached eight weeks of age, we introduced Eva to swimming. She seemed to enjoy the brief introduction to the warm water in the bathtub and especially enjoyed the towel drying that followed. A few weeks later we took her to a nearby pond. Our intent was to let her explore along the shoreline and possibly coax her into wading. If that worked, we intended to carry her out far enough that she had to swim at least a little bit. Well, surprise! She didn't explore...she rushed straight for the water and began swimming. There would be absolutely no problems except keeping her OUT of the water!

Hilde played with Eva constantly. Sometimes they

engaged in mock fighting and other times in tug of war with various toys or other objects. Hilde was always gentle and it was pure joy just to watch them play. If Eva tried to nurse, Hilde would gently discourage her at first and escalate to growls if Eva remained persistent. As time went by, Hilde spent less time training Eva and became more critical of Eva's actions. Of course Hilde utilized her teeth and her growl as necessary to register her disapproval. Simultaneously, Bobbie and I were interjecting our own ideas into the mix, but our emphasis was considerably easier on Eva!

Eva was a "chewer." We bought some *Bitter Apple* and sprayed her tongue with it, which definitely got her attention. Then we sprayed her various chew targets and it seemed to work well. We congratulated ourselves on our success. All of the toys and other objects that she was allowed to chew certainly received her attention. She was a puppy and puppies chew almost everything; most important, though, she was learning which items were okay to chew and rarely made a mistake...at least while she was young.

As Hilde decreased her playtime with Eva, the puppy began to lavish attention upon Blade. Hilde had initially communicated to Blade that the puppies were off-limits to him, but now he was considered a welcome member of the training team and she basically stopped training Eva. Don't get me wrong...she did NOT stop disciplining Eva! On the other hand, Blade did not do any of her training.

Another surprise: Eva was allowed to rest her head on Blade when she slept. We had assumed that Star was the only dog granted that privilege. It began as an occasional thing and soon became constant; if Blade was lying down, Eva would be using him for a pillow. They played together at every opportunity and soon were inseparable. Blade was particularly careful not to hurt Eva. She, on the other hand, was brutal and she had those sharp puppy teeth! It was such a ridiculous sight to see Blade using great restraint as Eva chewed on him. He looked so large and sounded ferocious, yet she was so small and her growl and bark were simply comical.

Eva was able to make Blade yelp at any time. He had a healthy respect for her sharp teeth, but still allowed her to chew on him. He chose to run away if she was particularly persistent, but would not even growl at her (other than in play). Apparently her companionship was worth the pain. As Eva grew, the bond became stronger. The absence of either dog had a profound effect on the other. Blade was affected more than Eva who was beginning to show a more independent attitude...clearly she was Hilde's daughter. Blade suffered from separation anxiety; Eva did not. She preferred his company above that of Hilde and though we hated to admit it, the same held true regarding us.

Eva was developing nicely. She was sleek, smooth and agile like her mother. We chose to let her spirit run wild rather than apply too much restriction and discipline. She was looking very much like a candidate for the show ring and her feisty attitude could possibly give her the edge over the competition. We were reluctant to take the chance of toning her down too much. Blade had taught us the importance of attitude in the show ring.

Eva was also showing great interest in birds. There was the strong possibility that she would develop into a hunter. I let her retrieve a training dummy and she returned it to my outstretched hand each time. So at the tender age of three months, I took her to a game preserve for her introduction to quail. She picked up the scent before we even reached the quail pen and became excited. She could not see the quail, but knew where they were. She did not know what they were, but somehow knew that she wanted them. Instinct is a wonderful thing.

Following the advice of the owner of the game preserve, I clipped the outer wing feathers on one wing so that the quail could not fly. I then hid the bird and with Eva on a long leash, I walked her downwind of the quail. When she picked up the scent, I let her approach the quail and was amazed as she established a very respectable point. I returned her to the Blazer and moved the quail to a new location. On the next trial I removed the leash and let her walk alongside. When she picked up the scent, she refined the direction of the scent and went straight to the quail. This was the moment of truth. What would she do?

Eva picked up the quail, carried it to me and gently placed it in my hand. Up until that moment I had assumed that she would consider the quail to be her special prize. There had been no sound from the quail and it was not injured in any way. We did this eight times with identical results. I was elated. The ninth attempt was not so rewarding. Eva had become quite proficient at locating the quail and was completing this task at a faster rate each time. On this occasion, she picked up the scent and went charging up to the quail much too fast. When she slammed on the brakes, she fatally injured the quail. We ended the session at that time. Her instincts were good and she had a "soft mouth" which is an important quality in any dog that retrieves game. This was without benefit of any training; this was pure instinct. I was pleasantly surprised and anxious to see her hunt with Hilde, but that was in the distant future.

Eva was almost six months of age when Bobbie returned from work only to find her with a severe bite wound on the left side of her chest. There was a round section approximately the size of a silver dollar where the skin was missing. It was possible to view her rib structure and related tissue which resembled a side of pork ribs. When the vet finished, Eva had a "T" shaped repair almost four inches long in both directions. She also received a special wide collar which would preclude any attempts to lick the wound.

We assume that Hilde did the damage since there were no witnesses...at least none that could talk. Since Hilde had never done any serious damage to either Blade or Eva, it was possible that Hilde had issued punishment for some transgression. At that instant Eva must have gone totally submissive and dropped to the ground. If Hilde's front legs were set and unyielding, perhaps that was enough to do the damage. On the other hand, maybe that is just the rationalization of the owner of a dog that has just severely injured another dog.

Chapter 32

Safety Day - 2001

Our portion of Safety Day 2000 at the power plant had been a success primarily due to the content of the presentation and the presence of Blade and Hilde. I was asked if we would be returning and decided that it would be a chance to pick up where we had left off. Of course this time there would be three dogs. It was going to be spectacular. Yes, it would be truly spectacular!

Safety Day 2001 was originally scheduled for mid-September. This was altered by the tragic events of September 11. Subsequently, Safety Day was canceled and then was re-scheduled for a late-October date. Numerous security changes resulted in the elimination of all outside demonstrations and displays by the various vendors as well as by the police and fire department. All presentations would be held indoors and our portion would take place in a large training classroom. We had received permission to have the dogs off leash.

The room had a door up front and another in the rear...a perfect set up. Chairs were to be placed so that only a center aisle was available. Warnings would be placed near the two doors advising that one or more dogs would be loose at various times during the presentation. Those personnel who were uncomfortable around loose dogs or those who feared dogs were not required to attend the session. Of course, they were welcome and could choose to sit near the walls and away from the aisle. A desk at the front of the room served as a stage for several demonstrations and was fitted with a special cover to ensure safe footing for the dogs. Many of the attendees had seen and met Hilde and Blade at the previous Safety Day or during other visits to the plant.

There was no reason to fear either of the two and Eva was just a puppy.

As Safety Day approached, I took each dog out to the plant on an individual basis and let him or her become familiar with the room. I let them wander around loose and gave them treats and even played some of their games until I felt that they were comfortable with this whole new environment. Hilde received a dress rehearsal and performed all of her requirements without any problems. One item could not be rehearsed since it required a member from the audience.

Safety Day finally arrived and the chaos began. I had taken most of the required gear and equipment out to the plant the night before to make things easier; three dogs and three crates would be plenty to deal with! The dogs sensed that something unusual was happening when the alarm clock awakened us much earlier than normal. Eventually, everything was done and the crates and dogs were loaded into the Blazer. Upon arrival at the Security Checkpoint, I produced my ID and lowered the rear window so the Security Officer could check the interior. Hilde greeted the surprised man who, with a huge grin, asked if they had ID. Imagine his surprise when I produced a photo ID for each dog...the look on his face was priceless! I did not bother to explain that IDs were part of the presentation.

I was able to recruit a helper and moved the crates and dogs into the classroom after several trips. Initially, their three crates were located at the front of the room. This was to preclude any anxiety by any or all of the dogs in this new environment since they would be able to see me at all times. The presentation would begin with a quick self-introduction and introduction of my helper and co-worker Cindy. The dogs had since been moved out into the hallway and brought to the rear door. We enlisted the assistance of one or two helpers who would release the dogs when directed. A video was the first item in the presentation. At a certain point it would be stopped and replaced with the "live action" portion which included some audience participation. The video would then resume and conclude the presentation. This procedure would be repeated six times as the different groups rotated between this and the five other presentations. There would be approximately seventy to eighty personnel at each session.

The first disaster concerned the video...portions of it were damaged and had to be replaced at the last minute; unfortunately, the quality was not good. Starting off with an apology was certainly poor form and it turned out to be an indication of things to come. Yes, it would be spectacular.

"Roll the video." Blade kicked off the video by stating the station's motto. (Of course he didn't REALLY state the station's motto.) A patriotic theme was followed by a welcome, a smattering of statistics and a review of canine aggression items filled the screen for several minutes and then stopped. From the rear of the room in order as called, came Hilde followed by Blade and Eva on a leash held by Cindy. This was accompanied by a lively rendition of "Who Let The Dogs Out?" which brought a few chuckles. It also was a little startling to those seated along the aisle as the first two dogs rushed to join their master and renew their acquaintance. I told the dogs to "settle" as I picked up Eva and placed her on the desk. First of all, they DIDN'T SETTLE and I was concerned with Eva and her new stitches. The reunion seemed to have no end in sight so I deviated from the plan. I told the dogs to sit and they did. I introduced each dog and gave a little background on them. I discussed dogs plus food plus jealousy plus conditioning. I then proceeded to hold a treat between my lips and offer it to each dog with a "no." There were no takers. Then I repeated it with an "okay" and each treat was gently taken from me. Medical personnel breathed a sigh of relief (and so did I).

I told Blade to get into his house and he immediately jumped down from the desk and entered his crate. Cindy held Hilde while I turned Eva so that the audience could see her stitches. I gave my theory on how the injury occurred and Eva garnered the sympathy vote. We put Eva into her crate and Hilde jumped up on the desk. It was the moment of truth. And it was going to be spectacular.

Part of the plan was to demonstrate several capabilities of dogs involving memory and response to voice commands and hand signals. Memory would involve placing two toys on opposite sides of the room while Hilde watched. Then a volunteer would be selected to approach and greet Hilde while the audience evaluated the results utilizing information presented during the previous Safety Day. The next phase would be to introduce the individual to Hilde by name, repeating the name several times. The volunteer would then return to his/her seat. Hilde would be commanded to go retrieve each of the toys previously mentioned. Once that was completed, Hilde would be directed to go to the volunteer using only the name of the volunteer.

Hilde would then be sent to find a treat being held by a designated member of the audience. Hilde would next be commanded to "stay," "down" and "come." After that, she would be taken down the aisle to the rear of the room and given hand signals for "sit," "down" and "stay." I would return to the desk and give the signal to "come." We would then revisit some of the DOs and DON'Ts regarding aggressive and submissive behaviors. Hilde would be replaced by Blade as the featured dog for the next demonstration.

Hilde sat on the desk and calmly watched the two toys being placed. She enjoyed the introduction to the volunteer and watched Judy return to her seat. Surprise, the volunteer had correctly approached and presented the back of her hand for sniffing. (This is going well.) Now it was time for Hilde to retrieve the monkey toy. "Hilde, go get the monkey!" Off the desk and over to the monkey...the response was immediate. Halfway back she spotted the tennis ball on the opposite side of the room, dropped the monkey and stopped. (Uh oh) "Hilde, get the monkey." I repeated the command and watched as she tilted her head from side to side as if confused. (Okay, you win.) "Hilde, go get the ball." She walked over to the ball, turned around and looked at me. (Was that a wink?) Mentioning that it must be stage fright, I decided to avoid forcing the issue and sent her to "find Judy." Well, guess what! "Hilde, that's the lady that I introduced you to about five minutes ago!!" She did NOT go find Judy. Marvelous.

(Maybe she will go find the treat.) "Hilde, find the treat." Off she went and found the treat immediately. (Oh, so now you remember if there is food involved.) "Hilde, sit." She did. (Wow, two in a row!) "Hilde, down." She dropped onto her belly. (This is more like it.) "Hilde, come." She raced to the desk and hopped up as I patted the desktop. I escorted her to the back of the room and explained what was next on the agenda. She sat on signal, laid down on signal and after giving her the "stay" signal, I turned and walked to the front of the room. I faced Hilde and held out my arm and watched her tremble in anticipation. I gave the signal and she sprinted to me and jumped up on the desk. She had redeemed herself! I toyed with the idea of trying the monkey/ball/volunteer items again, but decided to cut my losses! And maybe the audience would forget about her failure to find Judy.

Blade was next. Blade had stopped responding to the "come" command more than a year before and we had invested in an electronic collar. The fact that he was an escape artist was bad enough, but living near a busy street made it critical that he come when called. The collar accomplished that without resorting to extremes. The sound that accompanied the electrical stimulation was something that he remembered. I placed the collar on Blade, walked him to the back of the room and told him to "stay." I explained how the training had been accomplished and that I would be touching only the button that generates sound and that it had been months since he had heard that sound. This would demonstrate how effective his memory would be...of course it would only really be accurate on the first trial. I returned to the desk, pushed the button and Blade rushed to the desk and hopped up next to me. I removed the collar and used him for several other demonstrations.

There was one last major demonstration. With all three dogs loose Cindy would play a tape with the sound of puppies in distress. I asked the audience what the results would be and received various answers. I assumed that the dogs would show curiosity and possibly slowly move toward the back of the room to investigate. They listened for approximately one second and then rushed to the source of the puppies' cries! Luckily no one chose that time to stand in the aisle. That reaction was a surprise and it WAS spectacular!

We crated the dogs and played the remainder of the video. It was a series of phrases with the word "dog" in them followed by dog or puppy photos, and then an injury caused by a dog attack. It drove home the point of the presentation. The tape ended with the "credits" and the first presentation was finally over.

It was time to make some adjustments. We moved the crates to the back of the room...that caused the "off duty" dogs to bark since they could hear me but not see me. "I need a couple of volunteers to hold these two noisy dogs." Also, the rush to the front of the room was suddenly dangerous since the dogs were now much more eager to return to my side. This was not a good thing on Safety Day. During the "find the treat" sequence, Hilde picked the one individual in the audience who was extremely uncomfortable around dogs and decided to see if she also held a treat. To make things worse, Hilde then refused to leave the woman alone!

I abandoned the memory items for Hilde altogether. Of course, Eva received the sympathy vote each time. Finally, the day ended. It had been quite an experience and one never to be repeated. The dogs had improved as they became more comfortable in their surroundings, but it was another lesson on the difficulty in predicting behavior under new and changing conditions.

Oh, by the way...one of the attendees summed up the presentation, "The SOUNDTRACK was SPECTACULAR!"

Chapter 33

Eva – Part 2

There are times in life when things just start to unravel. Eva was no exception only it was her stitches; they began to break loose and it was off to the vet again. This time when he finished, she had only a vertical set of stitches about four and one-half inches long. The vet had been forced to remove some of the scar tissue and this time it was guaranteed not to tear loose! By this time we were expecting Dr. Newman to build a new wing at the animal hospital and name it in Eva's honor; short of that, perhaps to purchase a new Mercedes.

She sported her special restrictive collar which was approximately four inches wide. It was not possible for her to get near those stitches. Healing was rapid and soon the stitches were removed. She was back to her old tricks almost immediately. She began to greet us like she greeted Blade: gentle bites to the wrists or arms. It was cute and relatively painless. As she grew, however, the bites became annoying. To avoid bites, you were required to say, "No bites" and there would be none. To forget to say it was to receive a bite. Poor Blade could not mouth the words!

Eva had grown enough and the constant "in and out" demands by all three dogs resulted in our decision to install a pet door for entrance via the cellar. The door we purchased was perfect for the dogs although it would be a little tough for Eva to negotiate at first. Once the pet door was in place we commenced teaching the dogs how to use it. Hilde was the first to use it and that made it easy for Blade to learn the process. Soon both dogs were using it regularly. Eva, on the other hand, just happened to make her first attempt after Blade made his exit and the flap smacked her right in the face. That was a major setback.

I used treats and even held the flap so that she could see what was on the other side of the door; she would not even attempt an exit. I toyed with the idea of crawling through the small door, but a little voice inside warned me that a fire department rescue would certainly end up in the local paper. Then, out of the clear blue, Eva simply hopped through the door. That was the end of that problem. And, she had already mastered going down the stairs. We now could allow the dogs to move from indoors to outdoors and back without human intervention. We could also close an interior cellar door and limit their indoor access to just part of the cellar. It was a good thing. Even severe weather would not be a problem with this new arrangement.

"Eva the Chew Machine" delighted in dragging chewable items all over the yard. It did not matter what the object was or to whom it belonged. She was forbidden (as were Hilde and Blade) to take toys outside and certainly outside objects were to remain there. As weeks passed and the pet door became easier for her to negotiate, she began to import various forbidden items. She brought in a 2x4 that was almost two feet long. I wish that I could have seen her maneuver that through the pet door! Soon tree branches of all lengths were appearing in the living room...there was no doubt where they had come from. As she grew, the larger the branches. Her record is a branch that measured just under eight feet in length. She was only able to bring it halfway up the cellar stairs before attracting Michael's attention. All three of us marveled that she could somehow bring it through the pet door much less pull it around a corner and drag it while backing up the stairs! But then you must understand Eva and obviously we don't!

Eva had another surprising habit. Lulu and Star had loved to play with those toys long abandoned by Blade and Hilde. The condition or age of the toy was of no consequence...to them it was a brand new toy. As we encountered toys which had been put aside, we would give them to Eva. Usually she would play with them quietly for awhile and then prance in front of Blade hoping to entice him to play; he usually refused, probably because he knew they were old toys! The newer, soft toys were fair game for all three dogs. Blade immediately demonstrated how to remove the squeaker (if so equipped) and the stuffing. Eva was a quick study and quickly mastered both techniques. And so on any given day you could plan on seeing large quantities of white fiber stuffing and a toy that was only a mere shell of its former self. If a day went by and no stuffing was strewn about the house, then you could rest assured that it was time for some new stuffed toys!

If Bobbie and I left the house and Michael was home, we would often leave the cellar open. Sometimes we would give a rawhide "chewy" to each dog as we were departing. Eva would usually bury her prize. The odd thing was that she refused to bury it outside. She would seek out the magazine stack, the dirty laundry basket or the clean laundry basket and bury the special object with great care. Then she would nervously guard it while trying not to divulge its location. When we returned from our errand, Eva would suddenly appear with her "chewy" and we would be amazed at her restraint and self-control. Previously, the other two dogs would steal it as soon as we left. Her solution was simple and effective. Sometimes it was necessary for her to re-locate it because of compromise or possibly just to move closer to her human pack members. Eventually, she would retrieve it and commence its destruction in our presence, knowing that we would not allow the other two any opportunity to take it from her.

Eva's penchant for leaning on Blade escalated to include sitting on him. Either position was acceptable to her depending on available space. Since Blade registered no objection, she was free to maneuver as necessary to achieve her desired pose. We have watched her back up to him and just sit on him. Other times she would simply crawl on top of him and go to sleep. Occasionally she would prop her shoulder on him with the front leg casually draped over his body in a very classy pose. If he was not available, she would lean against the armrest on the sofa or love seat and place her leg on the top edge with the paw draped over the end. This always brought either a chuckle or sometimes an outright laugh. She shared her mother's love of the spotlight and thrived on the attention she generated. And, of course, we have photos!

Eva quickly learned that the Blazer was meant for trips and the Envoy was off-limits to all dogs. Hilde took special trips for hunting and Blade would ride with Michael to the dump. We managed to throw in some trips to include just Eva. On one occasion I picked up the Blazer keys and Eva went crazy. All week I had picked up the Envoy keys and she paid absolutely no attention. She had learned where the Blazer keys were kept and it was a possibility that she would be going for a ride. She knew that I drove the Envoy each morning and rarely drove the Blazer. This must be a special trip. Of course, she was unable to keep a secret and alerted the other two which resulted in three crazy dogs all intent upon exiting the front door. Talk about ruining a good thing!

Eva demonstrated other special knowledge. Bobbie came down with a severe kidney infection and during the recuperation phase was confined to bed for long stretches at a time. All three dogs remained close by, but Eva apparently realized that something was wrong. She sensed that Bobbie was ill and was very gentle when nearby. She spent a lot of time on the bed next to Bobbie possibly wondering why she had not gone to work. Suddenly, Bobbie was shocked to see Eva jump onto the bed with a slipper in her mouth. She initially scolded Eva for stealing a slipper to chew and removed it from her mouth. Eva left the bed and returned moments later with the other slipper and her tail was wagging fiercely. The message was clear: please get up!

Eva used her intelligence to manipulate Blade in numerous ways. If he was not nearby, she would "yip" in a manner that would bring him running to her. At that time she would indicate a desire to play and if he was not interested, she would persuade him by parading an array of toys past him until he gave in. She always won. If he was playing with a toy and she wanted it, it was hers in a matter of seconds. He would growl ferociously at her and she would completely ignore it and do whatever she chose to do. If Blade was gnawing on a beef bone and Eva wanted it she either took it outright or conned him with the old "Hey, come look at this" scam. At other times she just went over and chewed on him.

She took a perverse joy in shaming Blade into playing with her. She would pick up a toy and if Blade showed no interest, she would crash into him. She would repeat this until he growled at her and then she would do it one more time. That would be too much for Blade and he would chase her and the game would begin! I have never seen this tactic fail. Of course she had other talents.

Eva stole food from the kitchen counter. If it was not hidden, she would grab it and eat it. This never occurred while we were at home, only when we left. Even though Michael was home, she would be having a snack before we reached the end of our road. Those wooden, spring-loaded mousetraps turned out to be a wonderful choice. I purchased a dozen and set them in all areas where Eva preferred to "shop." These worked wonders, but they sure do hurt when you accidentally trigger one with your fingers! And it is an especially good idea to explain to company why you have so many mousetraps.

Eva's first choice for self-entertainment was always a trashbag. These she relocated to our bed and removed every single item. If the bag was too heavy to carry, she simply made multiple trips. Michael's greatest fun was the call to his mom's cell phone to ask her to guess WHICH DOG had found a WHAT and had spread it all over the bed. Sometimes he would ask her if she recalled seeing a trashbag in the house. That was sure to start the mind racing! Once he asked if there was any dip for Eva's chips. (Oops, forgot to set the mousetraps.) Possibly his most aggravating call was "I don't think I should tell you what Eva did." Now that was something to think about on the drive home (or all throughout the movie)!

There was one other item of special mention. Every dog has the strongest desire to be near its master. Eva clearly preferred Bobbie over me virtually all of the time. When separated from its master, a dog will often search for an article of the master's clothing, possibly as a way of trying to locate the master. Eva was no exception, but she was not content with the ordinary. Eva preferred Bobbie's bra and would gleefully take one into the yard to advertise to the neighbors how much she loved her master! We were not able to understand the why and how of her selection, but this happened numerous times. Clean laundry, dirty laundry...it made no difference. Only one person in the household failed to see the humor in it. I am smart enough not to mention her by name! Oh well, sooner or later she will read this!

Eva never carried any of my clothing outside, but settled for something else: my cell phone. She destroyed the case and then took the phone into the yard. Either she couldn't turn it on or thought it was broken and just left it outside. And now, if you hold it up to your ear and listen carefully, you can hear the sound of a dog breathing.

Eva acquired a taste for our sofa; she seemed to find the foam irresistible. It was impossible to catch her in the act of systematically destroying what had once been a very nice sofa. However, thanks to her I was able to see the huge amounts of foam and polyester padding contained in a sofa of that size. Lazyboy has an excellent warranty, but it does not cover dogs.

When it came to curing this bad habit, nothing worked, at least not on a permanent basis. Just when it seems that she has finally decided to stop the sofa destruction, she goes on a binge. We have given up and will see if Purina makes a dog food in "sofa" flavor. Maybe that will appease her until we come up with some plan other than locating a concrete sofa.

Chapter 34

Life With Three of 'Em

We have often asked ourselves why we needed the third dog. There is no simple answer. We really don't know. It seemed like a good idea at the time! Could we part with one of them...no! We must face the reality, however, that we will not have them forever. It is not a subject that we dwell on, but I think that each of us has briefly considered the loss of one of the dogs. That is something we will deal with at the appropriate time.

We have been asked how we can tell them apart. Yes, they are the same breed, but there is very little resemblance between them. I may have trouble with identical twins (the human variety) but the dogs are a different matter. Maybe it is simply the fact that we see them constantly or perhaps the three very distinct personalities make it easy. Regardless, we never get them confused.

Back in the old days when we had only Hilde, we just KNEW that she would be so much happier with a playmate. The dominance issue with Bailey next door had not changed our mind. Of course, now we know that Hilde did NOT require a playmate and would have preferred to be the sole dog in our household. We, therefore, had justified our desire for another dog as something special for Hilde. We had a whole host of reasons why the second dog would be a wonderful thing and very few, if any, reasons why the second dog would not be a good thing.

Somewhere in this gross rationalization was the amount of extra work generated by the second dog; there would not be TWICE the work. There is some truth there. For example, if you intend to scoop up some dry dog food from the container, you make only one trip rather than two. The same for water. Yes, you must get MORE, but it is still just ONE trip. The accumulation of solid waste in the yard is TWICE as much, but again, you only need to go out the door ONCE and re-enter ONCE after the clean up.

The cost of dog food, toys, collars, etc. doubles, but it is still ONE trip to the store. And, of course, the new crate: oops, that is a special trip, but then you must only do that ONCE. So, in our naïve method of calculation, the second dog is a bargain simply because you get more of everything good without an equal amount of bad. This is how we achieved equilibrium. Life became stable and maybe a little too tame.

Then, all at once, there we were with Hilde and Blade and a litter of nine puppies. Some way, somehow, we convinced ourselves that a third dog would result in even better economies of scale. That is when we should have sought psychiatric help. Perhaps we considered it, but lost our direction and decided that we MUST have one of those puppies. After all, we were entitled to one of the pups as part of our co-ownership agreement. Okay, same drill...THREE DOGS could not be much more work than TWO. Now if you honestly believe that...!

Yes, it IS two less trips to the food container and all of that verbiage that you read just a few seconds ago. Somehow, though, the equation changes drastically with three dogs. It turns out that the extra work level increases by a factor of at least 1.5 with the addition of that third dog. That negates any gain that was realized by having TWO instead of just ONE! In business this is known as "the point of diminishing returns." This realization comes a little too late in the game or at least it did in our case.

Luckily, Eva was simply overflowing with personality. This was certainly a major factor as we repeatedly asked ourselves what we were thinking when we considered adding the third dog. Blade and Eva had bonded and that was good; Hilde was independent and that was good

214

unless it resulted in someone requiring a trip to the vet for repairs! These three dogs did not work well together. There are no doggie games for three...just two. Jealousy was always a consideration when it involved food, toys, bed, sofa or proximity to the human members of the pack.

Regardless, Eva knew how to generate sympathy by either expression or action. I have never seen a dog that can look so pathetic. If that expression doesn't achieve the desired results, she uses other body language such as leaning against something and glaring out the corners of her eyes at the one who offended her. While that may have little or no effect on the alleged culprit, she garners the sympathy of any nearby humans. It works and she knows it. She is the perfect con artist.

Bedtime is a challenge due to the multiple steps involved. One must only ask, "Who needs to go make?" That prompts all three dogs to rush to the back door ready to do their business. Then they return and head for their crates if the living room lights have been turned off, or for the sofa if the lights are still on. Turning off the television is their official cue to go to bed.

Each dog knows that it will receive a small treat in its crate and that is part of the ritual. If the last person to go to bed has not appeared (with the treat) within a reasonable time, Eva will rush to find that individual to remind them of their responsibilities. If that ploy does not work, she goes back and enlists Blade's help. Once the goods have been delivered, she goes through an elaborate and very noisy routine which ends when she is finally down for the night. Hilde and Blade just go to their crates and patiently await their treat.

Since dogs have such an incredible sense of time, all three know approximately (within two minutes) what time the alarm will sound. This is fine except on weekends. Dogs have no concept of a five-day workweek; like some employers they expect the same thing all seven days. Eva took some time before she could last the entire night without needing to go out. Of course, Hilde and Blade were more than happy to accompany her, but we found that on those occasions they pulled the "we are going to bed, where's our treat" scam. So we simply told the two older dogs to go back to sleep and they did. Then we let Eva out. Without their support, Eva would not demand a treat.

Eva's ability to "hold it" increased until she only needed to go out approximately one hour prior to the alarm. When Eva tells you she needs to go out, you had better listen. One of us would get up, let her out, let her in and then try to put her back into her crate. Once, we made the mistake of just letting her hop up onto our bed and lie down. She immediately fell asleep and that soon became the norm and allowed us to go right back to sleep. However, I vaguely recall that during one of those barely awake situations, Eva simply hopped up onto the bed and went to sleep without benefit of the potty run. Shame on us. We allowed it and it became a routine. It slowly dawned on us that she could now "hold it" all night.

Back to the weekend routine. Two minutes before the alarm would have gone off had it been a weekday, three dogs would begin stirring. Bobbie and I initially tried to ignore them and that worked for a few weeks. Then they began to whine as if they needed to go out. That was our cue for action: we told them to go back to sleep! That usually bought us twenty or thirty minutes of additional sleep.

After that, the dogs would raise the stakes and we would be forced to let them out of their crates. At that point, either they would head for the backdoor or straight for the bed! Regardless, they would always reach the bed before their benefactor returned. That unfortunate individual would find it nearly impossible to regain his/her previous sleeping posture due to the three dogs. Of course, the lucky individual who had feigned sleep or was told to remain in bed also suffered. At least one and probably two dogs would take positions which would force the human member of the pack to assume positions which the human anatomy does not tolerate well. Consequently, sleeping late on weekends was a painful experience which was sometimes endured and sometimes resulted in an early breakfast for all.

Three dogs usually expend a tremendous amount of energy during the days, but they still require some extended, aerobic exercise. This is extremely beneficial to them and it is especially good for their owners. In warm weather we would take them to one of the nearby ponds for an extended workout. We would let Hilde and Eva retrieve toys without need for leashes. Both were only interested in swimming out, grabbing the toy and bringing it back so that the process could be repeated. The problem was that we had to separate Hilde and Eva since their drive to retrieve was so strong that we were forced to restrain one so that the other could make the retrieve. Eva would forget who Hilde was and would attempt to take the retrieved item from her...foolish girl!

As they tired and realized that they would have numerous retrievals, we were able to allow them to compete for the same item. The sight of the mother and daughter retrieving the same object was enough to bring a smile to anyone who witnessed the act.

There was one occasion where Eva took Hilde's retrieval toy from her and was rewarded by being held underwater for several seconds! The sight of only Eva's four legs sticking out of the water was a strong reminder of Hilde's commitment to good order and discipline. Of course, Hilde's head was submerged and bubbles flew from the mouths of both dogs. No repeat performance was required!

Blade was always restrained by a long leash. He would sometimes just decide to swim to the opposite side of the pond. We do not know why. As he grew older and started his stalking of the ferocious shrews and squirrels, we assumed that we were witnessing the beginnings of his hunting desire and assumed that he would soon show interest in birds. He did, but not as we had anticipated. He developed a strong awareness of birds that flew anywhere in the vicinity of the pond. If he was swimming at the time, he immediately went after the bird. He is a very efficient swimmer, but has yet to catch one of his target birds. He still sees this as a challenge and thus the long leash remains part of Blade's swimming attire. Ironically, he ignores flying birds at all other times.

More moderate weather brings opportunities to take all three dogs to nearby Miles Standish State Forest. Here all three can be turned loose and allowed to hunt. Actually, Hilde starts hunting, Eva plays at hunting and Blade runs around marking "his" territory and looking busy. Regardless of their actions, they work or play hard while I orchestrate the overall program. Eva eventually becomes more serious in the "hunting" process and Blade even falls into a half-hearted "hunting" routine. Finally, as their energy levels drop, I recall them and we return to the Blazer in a small, controlled group. They are usually asleep by the time I start the engine. These workouts have a surprising effect on both their physical and mental states. Dogs DO suffer from "cabin fever."

****

Are we obsessed when it comes to our dogs? Of course we are! There is a line somewhere that should not be crossed, but we don't know exactly where it is. To a person who does not like dogs, that line would be very close by; the line would move out a little bit more for someone who simply tolerates dogs. Both of the aforementioned would probably consider us to have already crossed that line. We would vehemently disagree! We certainly cater to our dogs and we spend excessive money on toys, but we do draw the line at doggy clothes. And boots and raincoats!

Well, actually I do have three shirts that glorify the breed. There might even be a couple of calendars with a few gray dog photos somewhere in the house. But that unique stationery and certainly those screen savers and backgrounds cannot be held against us. Of course that paw-shaped doorbell switch mounting plate was never installed, so that doesn't count. Lastly, that doormat with the pawprints and Weimaraner head and the words "Wipe Your Paws" was a gift from daughter Debbie and I wouldn't part with that under any circumstances. Otherwise, I consider us to be perfectly normal.

Chapter 35

Some Things We Have Learned

Raising one, then two and finally, three dogs has been quite an experience. Had this been our original plan, things would have been completely different.

One of the first things we learned was that the puppy stage involves much more than just watching a puppy grow. It involves a huge investment in time and it seems to last forever. For that reason, it helps if research is done in advance. Training a puppy is not difficult, but it must be structured. Plenty of assistance is available through books, but keep in mind that one book is not enough. Check several since there are many ways of accomplishing the same goal and each author has his/her preferred methods. It is far better to start correctly than to correct bad habits! And no two dogs learn the same way.

Socialization between the puppy and people plus the puppy with other dogs is vital. This must occur at an early age and continue. Above all, the puppy must learn that it always ranks below all human members of its new "pack." Any indication of aggressiveness toward humans must be dealt with immediately.

It is a good plan to enroll your puppy in "puppy kindergarten" which is available at most pet stores. Later, it may be wise to add additional obedience training. If obtaining a puppy from a breeder, ask about these types of training. If the puppy is a candidate for the show ring, the breeder may prefer to provide some very precise guidance on how to proceed.

Commands should be short and simple. All family members must utilize the same commands. "Off" and "down" have two very distinct meanings. We use "wait" which means that we are opening a door and the dog is not allowed to exit or enter. "Stay" would be inappropriate since it normally requires a release command. Consistency is the key and it makes life easier for all concerned.

Nutritional needs of the puppy and certainly the adult dog must be considered at all times. Quantity and quality are especially important. Virtually all name brands will provide 100 percent of the nutritional requirements. "Designer" brands do not necessarily provide greater nutrition, but will put a larger dent in your pocketbook. Snacks, whether for training or for rewards, should also be nutritionally complete and MUST be considered in the daily feeding plan. It is easy for a dog to gain weight...it's all about food and exercise, sound familiar?

Some dogs do not tolerate changes in diet or water. This can wreak havoc on trips if substitutions are made. Fortunately, our three dogs have never had difficulty in switching food or water supplies.

Dogs break wind. Sometimes these little surprises can peel the paint right off the walls or at least cause the room to be vacated! More than one poor dog has been sent to the pound due to this problem. There are additives similar to *Beano* which will achieve essentially the same results in dogs. Switching to a lamb and rice formula may also do the trick. Ask your vet. Life is so much better without this problem. If any of our dogs break wind, they immediately look at the nearest human to see if they will be the focus of some special attention!

A trip with three dogs results in a series of events. Hilde, as the canine matriarch, takes her pick of resting locations in the Blazer. She usually chooses to be next to the barrier. Blade takes the very back of the Blazer with his back to the tailgate. This provides the maximum distance from Hilde's teeth and gives him something solid to rest against. This is one area where he does not defer to Eva. She takes what is left. They usually lie down as soon as the vehicle moves.

Slowing the Blazer significantly results in three heads popping up and a turn onto a rough road will have all three on their feet and ready for action.

If the Blazer is parked, the three pass judgment on anything that approaches within fifty feet. People attired in black clothing are automatically suspect and will usually generate at least one bark. A black dog will have the same effect while other colors will receive less attention.

Finally, Eva has become protective of the Blazer while it is in motion. Motorcycles must not approach within one hundred feet or she starts to bark. She can be silenced, but not if the motorcycle gets within approximately thirty feet. An automobile at that same distance creates the same reaction. Now if she could use binoculars and just keep an eye pealed for state troopers!

****

Dog shows are a mystery to most people. Do not confuse a local show with the pomp and pageantry of the Westminster Kennel Club show. Often the general public is unaware of a nearby show and loses the opportunity to see what appears to be a huge and confusing canine zoo or circus.

In addition to the sheer number of breeds represented, the obedience classes demonstrate what a trained dog is capable of achieving. This is often a humbling experience for the average dog owner. The conformation classes are difficult to follow, but knowledgeable people are usually willing to explain what is going on. If you are a veteran of dog shows, help get the word out and tell your friends and neighbors to attend and to take a camera.

There is a final item that dogs have taught us: do not take yourself too seriously. A dog will assist you in making a fool of yourself and yet will not pass any judgment on you for doing so. No matter how hard your day has been, a dog will provide instant therapy by just showing you how glad he/she is that you have returned. If Hilde senses that something is amiss, she will move as close to you as possible and look you right in the face as if to ask what is wrong. Whatever the problem may have been, it recedes into the background because of her simple intervention. Blade has a different style: he simply comes over and lays his head in your lap as if to say, "Everything is fine." Eva comes over and BITES you...she is still a little rough around the edges!

I never intended to become attached to another dog and certainly not to three of them. But now I do know that time and money are of no concern when it comes to the welfare of these three wonderful animals that came to live with us...as part of our family. They are not "just dogs."

An Afterthought

Over the last few years we have been inundated with all sorts of items involving Weimaraners. These come from dear friends and acquaintances and include items such as magazine articles, news clippings and calendars. We have also received various William Wegman items including some of his photo books. We have even received phone calls telling us about a television commercial featuring the breed or even notification of a dog show in progress. We have enjoyed these treasures immensely.

One of the most appreciated items, though, was the following:

THE RAINBOW BRIDGE

Just this side of Heaven is a place called Rainbow Bridge. When an animal dies that has been especially close to someone here, that pet goes to Rainbow Bridge. There are meadows and hills for all of our special friends so they can run and play together. There is plenty of food, water and sunshine, and our friends are warm and comfortable.

All the animals who had been ill and old are restored to health and vigor. Those who were hurt or maimed are made whole and strong again, just as we remember them in our dreams of days and times gone by. The animals are happy and content, except for one small thing; they each miss someone very special to them, who had to be left behind.

They all run and play together, but the day comes when one suddenly stops and looks into the distance. His bright eyes are intent. His eager body quivers. Suddenly, he begins to run from the group, flying over the green grass, his legs carrying him faster and faster.

You have been spotted, and when you and your special friend finally meet, you cling together in joyous reunion, never to be parted again. The happy kisses rain upon your face; your hands again caress the beloved head, and you look once more into the trusting eyes of your pet, so long gone from your life but never absent from your heart.

Then you cross the Rainbow Bridge together....

- Author Unknown -

ISBN 155395747-4

9 781553 957478